Religion in America

SEMINARY ADDRESSES

&

OTHER PAPERS

Solomon Schechter

ARNO PRESS & THE NEW YORK TIMES

New York 1969

Reprint edition 1969 by Arno Press, Inc.

*

Library of Congress Catalog Card No. 79-83435

*

Reprinted from a copy in the
Columbia University Libraries

*

Manufactured in the United States of America

SEMINARY ADDRESSES
AND OTHER PAPERS
S. SCHECHTER, M. A., Litt. D.

SEMINARY ADDRESSES
AND OTHER PAPERS

BY

S. SCHECHTER, M. A., Litt. D.

PRESIDENT OF THE JEWISH THEOLOGICAL SEMINARY
OF AMERICA

CINCINNATI
ARK PUBLISHING CO.
1915

TO

DOCTOR CYRUS ADLER

PRESIDENT OF THE DROPSIE COLLEGE
COLLEAGUE AND FRIEND

PREFACE.

The following pages, representing a selection of Papers and Addresses delivered on various occasions, were intended to appear in the form of a volume some three years ago in commemoration of the Tenth Anniversary of the re-organization of the Jewish Theological Seminary of America. Illness and other untoward circumstances prevented me from giving my attention to their publication until lately. But it is this delay which made it possible to include the last five papers.

These papers lay no claim to the attainments of rhetoric, which are unfortunately beyond my powers, nor will the reader find in them any indulgence in abstruse learning, which, even if it were within my reach, would be out of place in popular Addresses like these. The references to Rabbinic literature were mostly omitted for the same reason. All I endeavored to do was to express my thoughts in plain and direct language, in which I hope I did not entirely fail.

Generally speaking, the burden of these Addresses, mostly delivered on Commencement and other fête days of the Seminary, may be described as a plea for traditional Judaism, which it is the mission of the Seminary to teach and preach in this country.

They protest against the "shock-tactics" of Higher Bible criticism; they plead for a better appreciation of Israel's past and a closer connection between this past and the present and the future; they demand a more thorough study of Jewish thought and Jewish life as deposited in our great literature; they insist on the development of Jewish science which would enable us to compete with other institutions of higher learning; they also advocate a deeper devotion to the laws distinctly characteristic of the Jewish conception of holiness, leading to a more strict observance of the precepts of the Torah, and endeavor to make us sensible of the danger of incessant innovations which must in the end touch the very vital organism of Judaism.

At the same time, however, these Addresses often revert to the desirability of adopting in our studies all the methods which distinguish modern research from the mere erudition of olden times. They also set forth the necessity of the future Rabbi's receiving a proper training in secular subjects, as guaranteed by the degree of B. A. obtained in some College of standing, before wholly devoting himself to Jewish learning. The greater part of a rather lengthy lecture is devoted to proving that not only was the application of scientific methods to Jewish studies not incompatible with the spirit of conservative Judaism, but that it was largely con-

servative Jews, or at least, men indifferent to Reform
tendencies, who availed themselves of the scientific method and became subsequently the most
prominent representatives of the scientific movement, both by their zeal and their productions.

These Addresses being mostly directed to young
men at the solemn hour of their leaving the Institution to engage in the sacred calling of Rabbi, necessarily contain admonitions with regard to the special
virtues expected from the spiritual leaders in Israel,
such as humility, meekness, peacefulness and consider-
ateness. There is nothing new in these admonitions.
They have been repeated often enough, but this
very frequency shows the danger to which the "men
higher up" were exposed at all times; and the danger
has certainly not passed away in our time, when
those smitten with the disease of sensationalism find
ready response in a press prepared to satisfy their
vanity with all the means for publicity at its command.

Sometimes opportunity was taken in these Addresses to appeal rather to the community at large
than to our graduates. As an instance, it will suffice
to mention the graduation speech, headed: "The
Problem of Religious Education," in which the
crying need for a religious education, only accessible
to the few, and even to these, in a very perfunctory
and unmethodical manner, was emphatically pointed
out. I may say that it is one of the merits of the

Seminary, to have been among the first public.
bodies which tried to grapple with this problem and
it is highly gratifying to me to see that the community did not remain quite indifferent to our appeal,
so that a regular religious educational movement
has been inaugurated almost all over the country.
It has not as yet worked miracles, but has already
effected some improvement in the methods of teaching Hebrew, and will no doubt, in the course of
time, make progress in the direction of religious
instruction, so that the danger of a Godless posterity
shall be averted.

As indicated above, the papers constituting this
volume are an expression of the conservative position occupied by the Seminary.   This conservative
spirit, I need hardly say, permeates the whole Institution.   It is taught by the Professors in the classroom; it is expounded in the pulpit by the majority
of our alumni; and is propagated by its friends both
in writing and by word of mouth on every occasion.

Not quite falling within the scope of this volume,
are the three papers to be named presently, treating
with subjects having little or no connection with the
Seminary or its policy.   The first of these is the
lecture delivered on Abraham Lincoln's Centennial,
forming a study in the spiritual make-up of the great
President, little discussed before.   How my views
will be accepted by Lincoln specialists is a question,

but whatever the answer, it is hardly necessary to remark that my conception of Lincoln's character is not an outcome of the teaching of the Seminary or its religious tendency. The second, is the paper entitled, "Rebellion Against Being a Problem," delivered more than ten years ago, containing political views with reference to certain events in past history, which are possibly not shared by my colleagues of the Faculty or by the friends of the Seminary at large. I still belong to that older world which accepted certain humanitarian principles handed down to us from the French Revolution as God-given truths, and which still looks upon the "Declaration of Independence," based on the same principles, as a sacred document in spite of all its "glittering generalities." These "glittering generalities" have built up the new world, while the so-called "eternal verities" or "realities" are destroying the old world. "And be it indeed that I have erred, my error remaineth with myself," and nobody else shall be made responsible for it.

The third paper is the one headed: "Zionism, A Statement," published in December, 1906, in which I explain the reasons for my allegiance to Zionism. But I should like it to be distinctly understood that this allegiance cannot be predicated of the Institution over which I have the honor to preside, and which has never committed itself to the Movement, leaving this to the individual inclination of the students and Faculty, composed of Zionists, anti-Zionists, and indifferentists. Speaking for myself, Zionism was, and still is, the most cherished dream I was worthy of having. It was beautiful to behold the rise of this mighty bulwark against the incessantly assailing forces of assimilation, which became the more dangerous, as we have now among us a party permeated by Christianizing tendencies, the prominent leaders of which are even clamoring for a recognition of Paul, the apostle to the heathen—not to the Jews. These tendencies, which it must be said in justice, would have been strenuously opposed by the founders of the Reform school, are now thrust upon us on every occasion, and Heaven knows where they might have landed us, but for the Zionist Movement which again brought forth the national aspect as a factor in Jewish thought.

But this dream is not without its nightmares. For in their struggle to revive the National Sentiment, some of the Zionist spokesmen calling themselves by preference Nationalists, manifested such a strong tendency to detach the movement from all religion as can only end in spiritual disaster. There _is_ such a thing as the assimilation of Judaism even as there is such a thing as the assimilation of the Jew, and the former is bound to happen when religion is looked upon as a negligible quantity. When

Judaism is once assimilated the Jew will surely follow in its wake, and Jew and Judaism will perish together. All this is a consequence of preaching an aspect of Nationalism more in harmony with Roman and similar modern models than with Jewish ideas and ideals. However, nightmares are fleeting and evanescent—the vision as a whole still remains glorious. The aberrations will, let us hope, be swept away quickly enough as soon as their destructive nature is realized by the majority of the Zionists whose central ideas should and will remain, God and His people, Israel.

Of a personal nature are the few obituaries reproduced here. They form a tribute to the memory of friends of which the American Jewish public, I am sure, has sufficient knowledge to honor their names.

In conclusion, I should only like to remark, that when reading these proofs it gave me special satisfaction to see that the conciliatory note is not absent from this volume. Standing as the Seminary does for the healthy development of traditional Judaism in the midst of many movements and vagaries none of which are without excesses, and against which we are constantly struggling, it was not possible that the controversial feature should be entirely eliminated from the volume. Yet it will be found that the ultimate goal at which we are aiming is union and peace in American Israel.

The union of which I am thinking is not one of mere organization. Organization is useful in the way of an auxiliary, but its saving virtues cannot be always relied upon. Whatever its effects may be for good, they are more than counterbalanced by its tendency towards materialization, resulting as history teaches in the de-secration, if not profanation of things holy. The union we are in need of, is one on principle and the recognition of vital facts, decisive in our past and indispensable for our safety in the future, by which alone Israel can hope for a "name and remainder upon the earth." Such a recognition, however, can only be brought about by a thorough knowledge of our great literature, in which alone the Jewish soul found shelter and expression for untold generations, joined to broad sympathy and loving understanding for all the aspirations and cravings and longings and hopes recorded in this very literature. This is the mission of colleges and Jewish learned societies. The longer I live in this country, the more I am convinced that it is only such a thorough and hearty union which will enable us to deal with the great problems, spiritual and otherwise, confronting us. Parties come and parties go, but the word of our God shall stand forever. And so shall Israel.

S. SCHECHTER.

CONTENTS.

THE EMANCIPATION OF JEWISH SCIENCE.*

S PEAKING is not my *metier*. I was brought up in
an atmosphere of silence, where people listen,
obey and occasionally also command. I am not
particularly proud of my incapability, as I never
boast of my shortcomings. I am only stating a sad
fact. Another fact is, that I came originally from
a place in which eating had little of the nature of a
sacrament and was never accompanied by solemn
speeches. Either the dinner was a success, and we
gave thanks with sighs of satisfaction for the good
things we received, or it was a failure, and we held
our peace in stoic resignation.

However, there is an old proverb, "If you come
to a place, follow its customs," and I mean to follow
them. In fact, except such trifling things as ice water
and certain articles of a rather theological nature
which I cannot well digest, there is no country whose
manners and customs, whose institutions and conceptions of right and wrong, I should more like to
adopt and make my own than those of this great and
free Republic. It was the dream of my childhood
ˇwhen I learned, through the *Sepher Haberith* and the
letters of Hag Vidaver in the Hebrew weekly, *Hama-
gid*, of the existence of a continent on which, according to my simple conceptions, people should stand
on their heads, and who yet somehow managed to
walk erect and free and even move quicker and with

*Address delivered at the Judaean Banquet, May 29, 1902.

a surer pace than we, with all our drill of thousands of years. It became dearer to me when such books as the Stories of the Pilgrim Fathers and the Lives of Washington, Jefferson and Lincoln became accessible to me, whilst in later life American history and literature became a passion with me, so that I gave many an hour to your country which was due to Palestine, Egypt and Babylonia. I am thus prepared to adapt myself also to the institution of after-dinner speeches. In accordance with the good old Jewish custom, I will only, in the presence of this distinguished gathering, premise my address with the words: "With your permission, my superiors in wisdom and my masters in eloquence."

Now I have spoken of your great and free country. It will, therefore, not be out of place if I say that it rests with you to undertake the emancipation of which Zunz dreamed and wrote about eighty years ago. The emancipation of the Jews, he wrote, will never be complete until Jewish science is emancipated. That is to say, till Jewish learning and Jewish scholarship and the knowledge of its literature have become recognized factors in the march of human intellect; till Jewish science should occupy a position among other sciences worthy of its long history and its influence upon mankind, holding an independent place, resting on its own merits, free from all patronage of malicious theologians and sulky divines. This was a wish expressed, as I have said, some eighty years ago. But matters have improved very little since then. If possible, they have grown worse. For dependent as the o'd Jew was in his relations to the outer world, he never allowed earthly powers to encroach upon his spiritual domain, which made his real life. He would lend and borrow and buy the old clothes of the *poritz* (the lord of the estate), but when it came to his religion he was every inch a king. He had no mortgage on his liturgy; it was entirely his own, and he watched over his sacred literature with the tenderness and the jealousy of a lover. The reverse of the picture is not pleasant to dwell upon. I always have the impression, when I come to a synagogue or enter the study of a Jewish scholar, that we are something of spiritual "schnorrers."

Now, the first thing that we have to recover is the Bible. There is a story of a Catholic saint who was beheaded by his pagan persecutors, but, like a good saint, he took his head under his arm and walked off. You smile, and think it perhaps too much of a miracle, but a Judaism without a Bible is even a greater miracle. It would mean a headless Judaism, for, gentlemen, Judaism is not merely an ethical society placed under the auspices of Abraham, Isaac, Jacob, Moses and Aaron. Nor may you flatter yourselves that a few chapters of Lotze, a few chapters of ill-digested Kant, a few pages from Matthew Arnold's *Literature and Dogma*, seasoned with a little Stein-thalism and a shouting of Evolution—that terrible word which has wrought more mischief and produced more platitudes and conceits than the worst theology ever did, there being not a fifth-rate extension lecturer who does not feel himself the promise and fulfillment of all humanity—you may not think that such in-gredients will go for the making of Judaism.

Judaism is a revealed religion, with sacred writings revealing the history of the past, making positive demands on the present and holding out solemn promises for the future. And these sacred writings are the Bible, and they ought to be the possession of every Jew, interpreted and commented on in the Jewish spirit. I am in no way antagonistic to all that is modern. I confess that my sympathies for Wellhausen are not very strong and that I have a tolerable antipathy against "painted Bibles" and mutilated Scriptures. But I know that the demands of science are inexorable, and I yield to no one in respect for such serious men as Dillman, Kuenen and Delitzsch. But the question may be asked whether it is really all science that is claimed as such. My studies within the past years, which centered largely around the Bible, have convinced me that there is much in the higher criticism, which is at best theology of a kind, not philology and history.

But apart from this question there is another consideration. An old friend of mine once said to me, "Even if you are able to translate a Psalm, you understand only the Psalm but not the Psalmist." Now I put it to you, whether in a school where a man like Duhm, one of the oracles of higher criticism, can declare that the Psalms are all mere rancorous party pamphlets, the Psalmist is understood or not.

Another instance is the attempt by a majority of higher critics to eliminate the personal element from the Psalms—I mean the *ich* question. You will agree with me, I think, that our grandmothers and grand-fathers, who did read the Psalms and had a good cry over them, understood them better than all the professors. I am not pleading here for an orthodox commentary to the Bible, but there is a Jewish liberalism and a Christian liberalism and even from the point of view of liberalism let a commentary be written in the spirit of a Jewish and not a Christian liberalism. Remember that the Bible was not discovered by Cheyne and Wellhausen. We worked over it thousands of years before the Occidentals could read a Hebrew sentence correctly. And a Jewish commentary should give us the opinions of Rashi and Aben Ezra, Samuel Ben Meir, and others whose words very often appear in present manuals under the firm of Dillman, Delitzsch and Ewald. A Jewish commentary will also be free from such blasphemies as Jahveolatry, the "whimsical God of Israel," and similar offensive terms. And above all it must teach us that we are the fulfillment of the word of God, and that the Old Testament and the whole history of Israel are not a mere preamble to the history of Christianity.

But we ought not to be satisfied with the recovery of the Bible alone. There is a large field of Jewish post-Biblical history which is our own affair to provide for. All your universities and colleges do very little for it. You have probably heard the story of the French actress who appeared only in the first act, never knew what became of the hero in the fifth act, and so believed that the whole story finished with the incidental family quarrel, occurring at the beginning of the play, in which her role was placed. Now take Schuerer or Holtzmann or Hausrath and you will find that with them the history of Judaism terminates with the unfortunate quarrel which took place between the year thirty and forty of our present era. They never give a thought to the terrible tragedy and triumphs upon which the hero Israel but entered at that period; indeed, they think we have not survived the family quarrel.

But I hope that no Jewish theologian, to whatever party he may belong, thinks that the literature covering the period between the conclusion of the Canon and the last sermon "published by request" is superfluous and non-existent for the modern Jew. And let me tell you that I think that the reform party among us (I do not like the term "reform" Jews, which savors of schism) is as much in need of a thorough and real knowledge of Jewish literature in all its branches and departments as their orthodox brethren. Indeed, the orthodox Jew can always take his manual like the *Chochamath Adam* or the *Kizur Shulchan Aruch*, wherein everything that he has immediate need of is stated with an enviable precision. He does not arrogate authority to himself to legislate; whilst those who are aspiring to authority for change and selection, if they mean it well with Judaism, should know where its vital points are, and what they may touch with impunity and what would mean suicide, and this knowledge can only be got from Jewish history and literature. The frequent appeals to "prophetic Judaism" are largely verbiage; you cannot live on oxygen alone.

Perhaps you will allow me to conclude with a passage from the Zohar which I have often used before, and possibly many others before me, but it bears repetition. The story runs that a certain Rabbi once sailed in a ship. When the ship came upon the high seas, a storm arose and wrecked the vessel. Down it went; but the Rabbi was a saint, and, of course, a miracle happened. The vessel came out at the other side of the globe, and he found men engaged in prayer; but he did not understand them. It is supposed by the commentaries, which are still to be written, that the cause of his inability to understand them was that they did not pray in Hebrew. But even worse would it be if the religious literature of the Jews should not be accessible to all the Jews. And here in New York, where the West and the East meet in such close proximity, it is especially necessary if we are all to remain brothers on earth, as we hope to be in heaven, that our religious literature should be based on and developed from that Sacred Book and Sacred Language which have always been the means of communion between Israel and Israel, and between Israel and his God.

THE CHARTER OF THE SEMINARY.*

AMONG the regulations relating to the benedictions which the Jew is bound to utter on various occasions there is one running thus:

הרואה אוכלוסי ישראל מברך ברוך חכם הרזים

"He who sees a multitude of Israelites, says the benediction, Blessed be He who is the sage of all these mysteries." So far the Rabbis. By mysteries they do not mean those closet skeletons of which the author of "Vanity Fair" knew so much, and of which respectability, sometimes even decency, demands that they should remain hidden away in some dark recess. Judaism is not a religion that spies upon personal secrets; and least of all would they be distinguished by a blessing, the great rule being:

אין מברכין על הקלקלה

"Decay and decadence are not the special themes of thanksgiving." What the Rabbis meant here by "mysteries" was that diversity in feeling and variation in thinking which confer individuality and character upon each member of the species, to such a degree as to crowd our planet with as many microcosms as there are men and women, each governed by its own laws and moving round its own sun. It is this individualism which practically makes each man a profound and complete mystery to the other, and it was this mystery of individualism, or, as the

*Inaugural Address, delivered November 20, 1902.

Rabbis phrase it, "the unending variations of mind
and the difference of facial expression" registering
our emotions, that called forth the admiration of
the Rabbis and caused the institution of the blessing.

But nowhere is the force of this mystery more
deeply felt than in addressing an audience recruited
from the Jewish community of this great city of
New York. Like the first man (Adam) in the fable,
whose clay (constituting his body) was gathered from
the four corners of the earth, this community is made
up of the elements drawn from all parts of our globe.
But while the miscellaneous factor in the creation of
the race aimed, as it was fully explained, at making
man a citizen of the world, the same process has had
the very opposite effect with our community. Each
train of arriving immigrants has brought its own
idiosyncrasies and peculiarities, its own ritual and
ceremonies, and its own dogmas and dogmatisms, all
of which are struggling for existence and perpetuation,
thus converting the New World into a multitude of
petty Old Worlds. My stay in this country is not of
sufficiently long duration to justify any authoritative
statement on my part, but even so far as my short
experience goes I can safely say that New York alone
could furnish us with an epitome of all the Judaisms
or *Richtungen* scattered all over the world, ranging
from the precisionism and mysticism of the Far East
to the advanced radicalism of the Far West, in addition to the shadowy no-Judaisms hovering on the
borderland.

Such a community is indeed a mystery. And this
mystery has become perplexing; for it is amidst all

these Judaisms and no-Judaisms that my colleagues
and myself are called to create a theological centre
which should be all things to all men, reconciling all
parties, and appealing to all sections of the community.
If I understand correctly the intention of those who
honored me with their call, and if I interpret my
own feelings aright, this school should never become
partisan ground or a hotbed of polemics, making
"confusion worse confounded." The name of the
Holy One, blessed be He, is Peace, and the place
erected to His name, and to the cultivation of His
Torah, should, to use the figurative language of the
Rabbis, be the spot on the horizon "where heaven
and earth kiss each other;" while those, who study
there should in some way participate in, and, as it
were, anticipate the mission of Elijah, that was to
consist not only in solving the difficulties of the
Torah, and removing doubt, but also in bringing
back the forcibly estranged, arbitrating between
conflicting opinions, and giving peace to the world.

Divine, however, as the work may be—and it
could certainly not be accomplished without support from heaven—it is not entirely superhuman, for
the creation of which I have just spoken is not a
Creatio ex nihilo. The foundations are laid and the
materials are given.

I am thinking, in the first instance, of the sainted
Doctor Sabato Morais, the finest specimen of a
Jewish martyr—that is, one who lived, not only
died, as a martyr—whose very appearance was an
inspiration, and whose simplest utterance was a

stimulus to faith in God and His Torah. His name
will always be remembered for good as the founder
of the Jewish Theological Seminary. For this institution he lived and labored the last eleven years of
his life, during which he acted as President of the
Faculty, in which his spirit will always remain an
active and living force; the Reverend Doctor Alexander Kohut, the great Jewish scholar and author
of the monumental work *Aruch Completum*, the
greatest and finest specimen of Hebrew learning
ever produced by any Jew on this continent, who
acted for the last years of his life as Professor of
Midrash and Talmudic Methodology, and even
when death was already overshadowing him spared
himself not, and imparted instruction to the students
of the Seminary. I am further thinking of the
Directors of this institution. The modesty of these
Princes in Israel, which shrinks back from all publicity and adheres conscientiously to the great maxim
that virtue is and must remain its own reward,
forbids me to be explicit. But we may mention here
the names of those departed: Mr. Joseph Blumenthal, the President of the old Board of Trustees, to
whose signal devotion this institution owes to a
considerable extent its continued existence; Mr.
Leonard Lewisohn, a devoted Jew, one of our greatest
philanthropists, whose benevolence extended to two
hemispheres, and who was one of the first founders
of the reconstructed Seminary; Doctor Aaron Frie-
denwald, a scholar and a gentleman, who held the
office of Director, both in the old and in the newly

constituted Board, and whose interest in the institution only ceased with life itself. With the Son of
Sirach we should say:

> "For a truth these were godly men,
> And their hope shall not perish;
> With their seed goodness remains sure,
> And their inheritance unto children's children;
> Their memory standeth forth forever
> And their righteousness shall not be forgotten."

With such models of energy and conviction, of
activity and saintliness, the Seminary should not be
at a loss to continue the work which these great
souls have prepared and ripened.

It should, however, be pointed out that the
directors of the reconstructed Seminary have also
given us some excellent hints as to the nature and
character of the work before us. Their words are:

*"The Jewish Theological Seminary of America was
incorporated by a law of the State of New York, approved February 20, 1902, for the perpetuation of the
tenets of the Jewish religion, the cultivation of Hebrew
literature, the pursuit of Biblical and archaeological
research, the advancement of Jewish scholarship, the
establishment of a library and for the education and
training of Jewish rabbis and teachers."*

These words are taken from the Charter, forming
the constitution of the Seminary, but, like all consti-
tutions, this also may profitably be submitted to the
process of interpretation and expansion. This
method we call Midrash. To this Midrash the rest
of my address will be largely devoted.

Put into somewhat less technical, or rather less
legal terms, the ideals at which the Directors of this

institution aim are the promotion of Jewish learning
and the training for the Jewish ministry. By learning or scholarship we understand a thorough and
accurate knowledge of Jewish literature, or at least
of parts of it. The duty of accuracy, even in the most
minute details of a subject, cannot be shirked.
"Through my intercourse with great men," says
Humboldt in his *Cosmos*, "I early arrived at the conviction that without a serious attention to details
all generalizations and theories of the universe are
mere phantasms." I know that the acquiring of
details is a very tiresome and wearisome affair, and
may well be described in the language of the old
Rabbis: "The part of wisdom learned under wrath."
But, unfortunately, there is no "snapshot" process
for acquiring learning. It has its methods and laws,
as ancient as time itself, and these none can evade or
escape. "If a man will tell thee," the old saying was,
"I have found Wisdom, but labored not (for it),
believe him not." The probability is that he found
nothing worth having.

It is true that occasionally we speak of a "Republic of Letters," a term which may be interpreted
to imply that a certain freedom of treatment is
granted to genius. Apart, however, from the fact
that we are not all Shakespeares or Goethes, or even
Walt Whitmans, it should be remembered that
Republicanism does not mean anarchy. Bad grammar, faulty construction, wrong quotations and mis-
translations mean with the student in the domain
of literature what lawlessness and anarchy mean to
the citizen in common life. And much as we may
differ as to the eccentricities of a Walt Whitman,

I am sure that we will all agree that ignorance of the language of the sacred literature of Israel in persons undertaking to teach Judaism has by no means any claim upon our forbearance as the vagary of genius, and has to be opposed as objectionable and pernicious.

Not less objectionable than actual ignorance is artificial ignorance. By this I understand that peculiar attitude of mind which, cognizant of the fact that there were such things as the eighteenth century and nineteenth century, with their various movements and revolutions in all departments of human thought, somehow manages to reduce them to a blank, as if they had not been. My friends, they have been! There has been such a thing as a rationalistic school, though not all its members have been rational. There has been such a thing as a critical school, though not all its adherents have been real critics. Arianism of the vulgar sort, and Marcionism of the nineteenth century type, have had their share in this work. There has been such a thing as an historical school, although not all those who were of it interpreted history in the right way. All these movements are solemn facts, and they can as little be argued away by mere silence as pain and suffering can be removed from the world by the methods of Christian Science.

Mark, too, that there is no intellectual wave that breaks upon our mental horizon, which, disastrous as it may appear to us, will not have some beneficial effect in the end. It may wreak desolation when it comes; it may leave the beach strewn with loathsome monsters when it recedes, but at the same time it will

deposit a residuum of fresh matter, often fruitful
and fructifying. To give one instance from our own
history, I will only recall to your minds the Karaitic
Schism. Vile and violent were its attacks upon the
tradition of the Fathers, and the breach is not healed
to this very day, but it had also the blessed effect of
giving a wholesome impetus to the study of the Bible,
which resulted in producing a school of Grammarians
and Exegetes, and perhaps also of Massorites, such
as Judaism had never seen before.

Thus these movements may all contain grains and
germs of truth, or at least may provide the *nidus* for
the further development of truth, and with all this the
student must be made acquainted. What they have
to offer may not always be pleasant to hear, but this
must be accepted as a judgment of God, passed upon
us for allowing our inheritance—especially the Bible
—to be turned over to strangers. At the same time
the follies and extravagances, occasionally also the
ineffable ignorance displayed by some of the leaders
of these movements should also be exposed, for the
demand they make for blind faith in the hypotheses
they advance is even more exacting than that made
by the old orthodoxies, and young men should be
warned against their pretensions. "Even the youngest
amongst us may sometimes err," was the answer of a
master of Trinity College, Cambridge, to a forward
youth, and similarly I venture to express the possibility that even the "newest" among us may sometimes go wrong.

The crown and climax of all learning is research.
The object of this searching is truth—that truth

which gives unity to history and harmony to the phenomena of nature, and brings order into a universe in which the naked eye perceives only strife and chance. But while in search of this truth, of which man is hardly permitted more than a faint glimpse, the student not only re-examines the old sources, but is on the constant lookout for fresh material and new fields of exploration. These enable him to supply a link here and to fill out a gap there, thus contributing his humble share to the sum total of truth, which by the grace of God, is in a process of constant self-revelation.

I may, perhaps, point out in passing, as I did on a somewhat similar occasion, "that this passionate devotion to the study of ancient MSS., which you may possibly have observed in some students, has not its source in mere antiquarianism or love of curios. The famous R. Nissim Gaon, the correspondent of R. Sherira and R. Hai Gaon, the author of the *Mafteach*, says, in the introduction to his work: "And I entreat everybody who will profit by the study of this book to pray to God for me and to cause me to find mercy whether I am alive or dead." Nowadays we are not always in a praying mood. With Hegel, some of us believe that thinking is also praying. But the sensation we experience in our work is not unlike that which should accompany our devotions. Every discovery of an ancient document giving evidence of a bygone world is, if undertaken in the right spirit—that is, for the honor of God and the truth and not for the glory of self—an act of resurrection in miniature. How the past suddenly

rushes in upon you with all its joys and woes! And
there is a spark of a human soul like yours come to
light again after a disappearance of centuries, crying
for sympathy and mercy, even as R. Nissim did.
You dare not neglect the appeal and slay this soul
again.   Unless you choose to become another Cain
you must be the keeper of your brother and give
him a fair hearing.   You pray with him if he happens to be a liturgist;   you grieve with him if the
impress left by him in your mind is that of suffering; you fight for him if his voice is that of ardent
partisanship, and you even doubt with him if the
garb in which he makes his appearance is that of
an honest skeptic—"Souls can only be kissed through
the medium of sympathy."

But it is with truth as it is with other ideals and
sacred possessions of man.   "Every generation," the
ancient Rabbis say, "which did not live to see the
rebuilding of the Holy Temple must consider itself
as if it had witnessed its destruction."   Similarly we
may say that every age which has not made some
essential contribution to the erection of the Temple
of Truth and real *Wissenschaft* is bound to look upon
itself as if it had been instrumental in its demolition.
For it is these fresh contributions and the opening of
new sources, with the new currents they create, that
keep the intellectual and the spiritual atmosphere in
motion and impart to it life and vigor.   But when,
through mental inertia and moral sloth, these fresh
sources are allowed to dry, stagnation and decay are
sure to set in.   The same things happen which came
to pass when Israel's sanctuary was consumed in fire.

Said R. Phineas ben Yair: "Since the day on which the Holy Temple was destroyed, the *socii*, חברים sons of freedom, lie under the cloud of shame, and their heads are covered (in mourning); men of (real) deeds are neglected, while the 'men of elbow' and the 'masters of the tongue' gain strength."

I have thus far spoken of the Seminary as a place of learning. We must now proceed to consider it in its particular aspect as a training school for the Jewish ministry. Now, we all agree that the office of a Jewish minister is to teach Judaism; he should accordingly receive such a training as to enable him to say: "*Judaeici nihil a me alienum puto.*" "I regard nothing Jewish as foreign to me." He should know everything Jewish—Bible, Talmud, Midrash, Liturgy, Jewish ethics and Jewish philosophy; Jewish history and Jewish mysticism, and even Jewish folklore. None of these subjects, with its various ramifications, should be entirely strange to him.

Remember, my friends, that there is no waste in the world of thought. Every good action, the mystics say, creates an angel; and every real thought, it may be said, creates even something better; it creates men and women. In spite of all our "modernity," most of our sentiments are "nothing else but organized traditions; our thoughts nothing else but reminiscenses, conscious and unconscious," while in our actions we are largely executive officers, carrying out the ordinances passed by a wise legislation of many years ago. We dare not neglect any part of this great intellectual bequest but at a serious risk and peril to ourselves. And the risk is the greater in Jewish literature—a literature pregnant with "thoughts that breathe and words that burn," whose very pseudography became the sacred books of other nations, whose most homely metaphors were converted from literature into dogma. Nay, the very misunderstanding and misinterpretation of its terminology have given rise to a multitude of sects and orthodoxies and heresies still dividing humanity.

It is with the purpose of avoiding this risk that we—my colleagues and I—tried to draw up the curriculum of studies for the classes, in such a way as to include in it almost every branch of Jewish literature. We cannot, naturally, hope to carry the student through all these vast fields of learning at the cultivation of which humanity has now worked for nearly four thousand years. But this fact must not prevent us from making the attempt to bring the students on terms of acquaintance at least with all those manifestations of Jewish life and Jewish thought which may prove useful to them as future ministers, and suggestive and stimulating to them as prospective scholars.

It is hardly necessary to remark that the Jewish ministry and Jewish scholarship are not irreconcilable. The usefulness of a minister does not increase in an *inverse ratio* to his knowledge—as little as bad grammar is specially conducive to morality and holiness. Zunz's motto was, "Real knowledge creates action" (*thatenerzeugend*), and the existence of such men as R. Saadya Gaon and R. Hai Gaon, Maimonides, and Nachmanides, R. Joseph Caro and R. Isaac Abarbanel, Samson Raphael Hirsch and Abraham

Geiger, and an innumerable host of other spiritual kings in Israel, all "mighty in the battles of the Torah," and voluminous authors, and at the same time living among their people and for their people and influencing contemporaries, and still at this very moment swaying the actions and opinions of men— all these bear ample testimony to the truth of Zunz's maxim. No, ignorance is not such bliss as to make special efforts necessary to acquire it. There is no cause to be afraid of much learning, or, rather, of much teaching. The difficulty under which we labor is rather that there are subjects which cannot be taught, and yet do form an essential part of the equipment of a Jewish minister.

But first let me say a few words about the general religious tendency this Seminary will follow. I am not unaware that this is a very delicate point, and prudence would dictate silence or evasion. But life would hardly be worth living without occasional blundering, "the only relief from dull correctness." Besides, if there be in American history one fact more clearly proved than any other it is that "know-nothing-ism" was an absolute and miserable failure. I must not fall into the same error. And thus, sincerely asking forgiveness of all my dearest friends and dearest enemies with whom it may be my misfortune to differ, I declare, in all humility, but most emphatically, that I do know something. And this is that the religion in which the Jewish ministry should be trained must be specifically and purely Jewish, without any alloy or adulteration. Judaism must stand or fall by that which distinguishes it

from other religions as well as by that which it has
in common with them. Judaism is *not* a religion
which does not oppose itself to anything in particular. Judaism is opposed to any number of things,
and says distinctly "thou shalt not." It permeates
the whole of your life. It demands control over all
your actions, and interferes even with your menu.
It sanctifies the seasons, and regulates your history,
both in the past and in the future. Above all, it
teaches that disobedience is the strength of sin. It
insists upon the observance both of the spirit and of
the letter; spirit without letter belongs to the species
known to the mystics as "nude souls" נשמתין ערטילאין
wandering about in the universe without balance and
without consistency, the play of all possible currents
and changes in the atmosphere. In a word, Judaism
is absolutely incompatible with the abandonment of
the Torah. Nay, the very prophet or seer must bring
his imprimatur from the Torah. The assertion that
the destruction of the Law is its fulfillment is a mere
paradox, and recalls strongly the doctrines of Sir
Boyle Roche, "the inimitable maker of Irish bulls."
He declared emphatically that he "would give up a
part, and, if necessary, the *whole* of the constitution,
to preserve the *remainder!*"

President Abraham Lincoln, the wisest and greatest of rulers, addressed Congress on some occasion
of great emergency with the words: "Fellow citizens,
we cannot escape history." Nor can we, my friends.
The past, with its long chain of events, with its woes
and joys, with its tragedies and romances, with its
customs and usages, and above all, with its bequest

of the Torah, the great entail of the children of
Israel, has become an integral and inalienable part
of ourselves, bone of our bone and flesh of our flesh.
We must make an end to these constant amputations if we do not wish to see the body of "Israel"
bleed to death before our very eyes. We must leave
off talking about Occidentalizing our religion—as if
the Occident has ever shown the least genius for
religion—or freeing the conscience by abolishing
various laws. These, and similar platitudes and stock
phrases borrowed from Christian apologetics, must
be abandoned entirely if we do not want to drift
slowly but surely into Paulinism, which entered the
world as the deadliest enemy of Judaism, pursued
it through all its course and is still finding its abettors
among us, working for their own destruction. Lord,
forgive them, for they know nothing. Those who
are entrusted with carrying out the purpose of this
institution, which, as you have seen, aims at the
perpetuation of the tenets of the Jewish religion,
both pupils and masters, must faithfully and man-
fully maintain their loyalty to the Torah. There is
no other Jewish religion but that taught by the Torah
and confirmed by history and tradition, and sunk
into the conscience of Catholic Israel.

I have just hinted at the desirability of masters
and pupils working for one common end. You must
not think that our intention is to convert this school
of learning into a drill ground where young men will
be forced into a certain groove of thinking, or,
rather, not thinking; and after being equipped with
a few devotional texts, and supplied with certain

catchwords, will be let loose upon an unsuspecting public to proclaim their own virtues and the infallibility of their masters. Nothing is further from our thoughts. I once heard a friend of mine exclaim angrily to a pupil: "Sir, how dare you always agree with me?" I do not even profess to agree with myself always, and I would consider my work, to which, with the help of God, I am going to devote the rest of my life, a complete failure if this institution would not in the future produce such extremes as on the one side a raving mystic who would denounce me as a sober Philistine; on the other side, an advanced critic, who would rail at me as a narrow-minded fanatic, while a third devotee of strict orthodoxy would raise protest against any critical views I may entertain. "We take," says Montaigne, "other men's knowledge on trust, which is idle and superficial learning. We must make it our own." The Rabbis express the same thought with allusion to Ps. 1:2 which they explain to mean that what is first—at the initiation of man into the Law—God's Torah, becomes, after a sufficient study, man's own Torah. Nay, God even deigns to descend to man's own level so as not to interfere with his individuality and powers of conception. I reproduce in paraphrase a passage from a Midrash: "Behold now how the voice of Sinai goes forth to all in Israel attuned to the capacity of each; appealing to the sages according to their wisdom; to the virile according to their strength; to the young according to their aspiring youthfulness, and to the children and babes according to their innocence; aye, even to the women according to their motherhood." All that I plead for is that the voice should come from Sinai, not from Golgotha; that it should be the voice of Jacob, not of Esau. The Torah gave spiritual accommodation for thousands of years to all sorts and conditions of men, sages, philosophers, scholars, mystics, casuists, school men and skeptics; and it should also prove broad enough to harbor the different minds of the present century. Any attempt to place the centre of gravity outside of the Torah must end in disaster. We must not flatter ourselves that we shall be allowed to land somewhere midway, say in some Omar Khayyam cult or in some Positivists' society or in some other agnostic makeshift. No, my friends, there are laws of gravitation in the spiritual as there are in the physical world; we cannot create halting places at will. We must either remain faithful to history or go the way of all flesh, and join the great majority. The teaching in the Seminary will be in keeping with this spirit, and thus largely confined to the exposition and elucidation of historical Judaism in its various manifestations.

But, as I have hinted before, not everything can be taught. I am referring to those things undefinable, which may be best described by using the Talmudic phrase "things handed over to the heart," which cannot be imparted by word of mouth, or by any visible sign. Take, for instance, the Fifty-first Psalm, commencing "Have mercy upon me, O God!" We have the means of teaching how to parse the Hebrew and how to render it into fair English, but we are utterly helpless should we attempt to convey any idea of the agony and anguish which wrung from

the Psalmist this cry—of the misery and bitterness
which he felt at the thought that transgression and
sin may lead to his being cast away from the presence
of God, and to the loss of His Holy spirit; and of the
sudden exaltation and gladness he experienced in
anticipating the time when a broken heart and a
contrite spirit would bring back to him the lost joy
of salvation and restore the interrupted communion
between the repentant son and his Father in heaven.
Or take the concluding lines of the *Malchiyoth* benediction on New Year's Day that read: "Our God
and God of our fathers, reign Thou in Thy glory
over the whole universe and be exalted above all the
earth in Thine honor, and shine forth in the splendor
and excellence of Thy might upon all the inhabitants
of Thy world." We can easily lecture on the history
of this prayer, and even make a guess as to its date
and authorship, but we should certainly fail were
we to try to make one understand what the Kingdom of God on earth really meant for the saints of
Israel, whose whole life was nothing else than a preparation for entering into the Kingdom. Wooden theologians speak of a theocracy as a sort of Jewish
hierarchy after the Roman model, only with a Rabbi
Maximus as its head. This was not the ideal for
which so many noble men and women suffered martyrdom and which inspired the great "Unknown" to
his divine poem, ויאתיו כל לעבדך the Jewish "Mar-
seillaise." It was the blissful vision of love triumphant,
righteousness triumphant, truth triumphant, which
animated and dictated these lines. But here I am
explaining dark riddles by obscure terms. Or lastly,

take the first lines of R. Jehuda Ha-Levi's poem on
the advent of the Sabbath, running thus: "To Thy
love I drink my cup." The Sabbath was for him a
reality in which Israel's sweet singer saw a reflex of
the great Sabbath when the Kingdom of God would
be established. But how one can fall in love with
such an abstract idea as a span of time can only be
divined by love itself. In the famous Praise of Wisdom, Sophia or the Torah proclaims: "I am the
mother of fair love and fear and knowledge and holy
hope." But it is only filial devotion which will elicit
a mother's answer and touch the mystic chord of
things undefinable, only transmissible through the
means of an appeal from soul to soul. But suppose
a person has no soul, or, what comes to the same
thing, persuades himself he has none? "Saving souls"
is a favorite phrase with theologians. The soul
being, according to Jewish mystics—long before
Emerson—a spark of the divine essence itself, I
never believed it to be in much need of artificial aids
to salvation. The "Spirit shall return unto God who
gave it," even against the will of theologians if need
be. Our real difficulty is how to help the men without souls!

Another problem presenting itself is how we are
to teach the subject or thing called Life. I hardly
need say that by Life I do not understand skill in
arranging socials and other attractions, or ingenuity
in inventing sensational sermon headings. This is
not Life. Everything tending to what is common or
sensational must needs starve our better selves and
ultimately result in spiritual death. What I mean by

this term is the capacity for dealing with those occasions in our earthly career, which, by reason of intense joys or overwhelming sorrow or the tender sympathy which they evoke, crowd years into moments, and form, so to speak, portions of life in condensation. These occasions have always been controlled and assisted by religion. Of certain of these the Catholic Church has made sacraments, as in the case of marriage and death, and it has also created special Orders devoted to the work among the needy and the helpless. The Protestant Church has also its Settlements and has introduced into its seminaries pastoral theology, aiming, among other things, to instruct its clergy in the works of love and charity. But it must be confessed that we are still somewhat behind in this last respect.

Pray let there be no misunderstanding about this point. The discovery of the virtue of charity is not quite contemporaneous with the coining of that barbaric word Altruism. The administration of charity was one of the earliest functions of the Synagogue, from which it was borrowed by the primitive Church, like so many other institutions. But recognizing no difference between the laity and the priesthood, or "Rabbihood," the exercise of this function was not limited to any Order or special caste. The practice of the work of loving kindness, or *Gemilath Chasadim*, a term including everything we understand by philanthropic and social work, had, as you know from your prayer book, no fixed measure, and all classes of the community shared it. With regard to visiting the sick and ministering to the dying, I will only call to mind the oldest Jewish Society, the חברא קדישא a kind of Sacred Brotherhood, whose duty it was to nurse those who had nobody to attend to them, to be present at the supreme moment of man's existence, and to read the prescribed prayers there, to arrange and prepare for the funeral procession and decent burial, and to comfort the mourners by reciting prayers and "speaking to their hearts." All these services were performed voluntarily and gratuitously, and those who performed them came from all classes of the community, men and women.

But times have changed; charity has become to some extent—I hope not entirely—a science, and a certain knowledge of political economy and sociology is required for its proper administration. It is therefore deemed advisable that the minister, who, as a rule, is connected with our charitable institutions, either as an active member of the board of management or as the spiritual adviser of the directors, should receive some training in the aforementioned subjects, Again, we live now in the age of specialization. Funerals and burials have been raised to the dignity of a fine art, and praying has become a close profession. The old Sacred Brotherhoods thus had to disappear, and their work mostly devolves now upon the minister. But how should we approach this part of our instruction? It should be remembered that the old Sacred Brotherhoods were, as already said, voluntary societies, and the very fact of a man's joining them testified to his fitness to engage in the works of mercy and loving-kindness. But a man may show the most brilliant record of undergraduate days and yet be utterly wanting in tact, delicacy, patience, sympathy, forbearance and similar qualities necessary for the office of pastor. Sometimes a certain unwillingness to allow students to share in work of this kind is shown on the part of those who have a right to protest. The Jerusalem Talmud records a story of a famous Rabbi of Caesarea who sent his son to Tiberias "to acquire merit there" by studying Torah in the Rabbinic Academies of that city. But the youth, instead of attending to his lessons and lectures, became a "Gomel Chesed," or, as we should now say, devoted himself to social work. His specialty was, it seems, that of burying the dead. Whereupon his father wrote to him: "Is it because there were no graves in Caesarea that I sent thee to Tiberias?" This happened somewhere about the end of the third century, but in this respect times have not changed as far as my knowledge of universities and seminaries goes. Parents and guardians still object to their sons or wards attending funerals instead of lectures. But there is also another grave consideration. The social work included under the name of *Gemilath Chasadim* forms in Judaism a part of Israel's great *Imitatio Dei*. The Holy One, blessed be He, set the example Himself of performing deeds of kindness to His creatures, and it is incumbent upon the whole of Israel, "the suite of the King," as the ancients expressed it, to fashion their ways after the King. And I consider it not without danger to create a religious aristocracy which might soon claim the King entirely for themselves, and crowd the rest of us out from His Divine Presence. Such things have happened in other communities and may also happen to us when we create a separate class of *religieuses* with a special purpose of assisting us in the most sacred, but also the most sensitive and weakest, moments of our being.

George Eliot, in a letter to a spiritual correspondent, says: "The great thing is to do without chloroform." Judaism not only did without chloroform, but, retaining its freshness and vigor, it also did without crutches, and found its way to heaven without any aid from man: it never employed spiritual derricks. If a Jew wanted to pray, he prayed. If he felt anxiety about his soul, he said: "Into Thy hands I commit my spirit; Thou hast redeemed me, O Lord, God of Truth." If he felt the need of religious comfort, he read a Psalm or two and had a good cry over that, and he received assurance; and if he was in the home of a dying friend he read: "Hear, O Israel!" שְׁמַע יִשְׂרָאֵל and a few other verses acknowledging the unity of God and His reign, and he felt sure that both he and his departed friend would have their share in the Kingdom of Heaven. Now, on account of the frequent amputations, we have lost our vigor and have suddenly grown old and seem to be in need of artificial support, like other denominations. The support has to be created. The circumstances require it. But, as I have said, the experiment is risky, and we can only pray with the Psalmist that God lead us in the path of righteousness for His name's sake.

However, I will not dwell any longer on our troubles and difficulties. Be they ever so many, and ever so serious, the old dictum of the Rabbi still holds good: "It is not incumbent upon thee to finish the work, neither art thou free to desist from it," and least of all dare we desist from our work; we whom Providence has transplanted into this great and glorious country, and each of whom may verily say with Joseph, "God did send me before you to preserve life."

My friends, in a letter by Maimonides, addressed to the Wise Men of Lunel, there occurs a passage to the following effect: "Be it known unto you, my masters and friends, that in these hard times none are left to lift up the standard of Moses and inquire into the world of the Rabbis but you. I am certain that you and the cities near you are continually establishing places of learning and that you are men of wisdom and understanding. From all other places the Torah has utterly disappeared. The majority of the great countries are (spiritually) dead. The minority is *in extremis*, while three or four places are in a state of convalescence. * * * It is also known unto you what persecutions have been decreed against the Jewish population of the West (of Europe). There is no help left to us but in you, our brethren, even the men of our kindred. Be of good courage, and let us behave ourselves valiantly, for our people and for the cities of God, since you are manly men and men of power."

This letter was written by Maimonides some seven hundred years ago. But how little times have changed. Substitute the words East or Northeast for West, and you have the tragedy repeated before your very eyes. It is now the East—from our part of the globe—which is old and ill, where persecution has been decreed, and which, if not actually dead, is very nearly *in extremis*; while it is the West that is throbbing with life and healthy activity, which is full of men of understanding and wisdom, of power and of influence. To these I venture to repeat the words of Scripture in the sense in which they were used by Maimonides: "Be of good courage and let us behave ourselves valiantly, for ourselves, and for the cities of our God." Perhaps I may also repeat here another sentence of Maimonides: "Think not of thyself slightly, and do not despair of perfection." Whether we shall reach perfection in this or any other task relating to Judaism which the great men of Israel of this country have set before themselves, only the future can decide. But there is no reason for despairing; and the possibility of failure must in no way deter us.

There is a passage in the Talmud: "It is not a great honor for the princess when her praise comes from her friend; it should come from her rival." Ernest Renan, who never quite laid aside his St. Sulpice frock, and was never entirely free from Aryan prejudices, was certainly a rival, but he was a man of genius, and in spite of himself could not help occasionally saying true things; and his words are: "There will continue to be in Israel profound dreamers to assert that the work of God will never be complete until His true saints shall reign therein (in the world). At the root of the lofty morality of this people is a longing that is never satisfied. The true Israelite is he who, in his discontent, thirsts always for the future, and the race is not yet ready to fail." By the help of God we shall not fail.

HIGHER CRITICISM—HIGHER ANTI-SEMITISM.*

MY ACQUAINTANCE with Dr. Kohler dates from the year 1901, when he did me the honor of paying me a visit at Cambridge, England. There is no scarcity in that ancient seat of learning, "full of sages and scribes," of learned conversation. But the day with Dr. Kohler was one of the most delightful I have ever experienced in that place. The day was spent in roaming over the contents of the Genizah and in conversation. Our thoughts were turned to Judaism and the subjects which occupied our minds were all of a theological or historical nature. We probably differed in a good many points, and please God we shall differ in many more—but this did not prevent our short acquaintance from ripening at once into what might approach friendship. I felt that I was in the presence of a scholar and a seeker after truth. His is an intellect devoted entirely to what *he* considers the truth, and his is a heart deeply affected by every spiritual sensation which is in the air. He also delights to engage in what he considers the "Battles of the Lord," and Judaism has need for men of valor.

To speak more clearly: Since the so-called emancipation, the Jews of the civilized world have been lulled into a fancied security which events have not

---

*Address delivered at Judaean Banquet, given in honor of Dr. Kaufman Kohler, March 26, 1903.

justified. It is true that through the revelations in
the Dreyfus case, anti-Semitism of the vulgar sort
has become odious, and no lady or gentleman dares
now to use the old weapons of the times of Drumont
and Stoecker. But the arch-enemy has entered upon
a new phase, which Boerne might have called "the
philosophic 'Hep-Hep.'" And this is the more
dangerous phase because it is of a spiritual kind, and
thus means the "excision of the soul," leaving us
no hope for immortality. I remember when I used
to come home from the *Cheder*, bleeding and crying
from the wounds inflicted upon me by the Christian
boys, my father used to say, "My child, we are in
Galuth (exile), and we must submit to God's will."
And he made me understand that this is only a
passing stage in history, as we Jews belong to eternity,
when God will comfort His people. Thus the pain
was only physical, but my real suffering began later
in life, when I emigrated from Roumania to so-called
civilized countries and found there what I might call
the Higher anti-Semitism, which burns the soul
though it leaves the body unhurt. The genesis of
this Higher anti-Semitism is partly, though not entirely—for a man like Kuenen belongs to an entirely
different class—contemporaneous with the genesis
of the so-called Higher criticism of the Bible. Wellhausen's Prolegomena and History are *teeming with
aperçes* full of venom against Judaism, and you cannot
wonder that he was rewarded by one of the highest
orders which the Prussian Government had to bestow.
Afterwards Harnack entered into the arena with his
"Wesen des Christenthums," in which he showed not so

much his hatred as his ignorance of Judaism. But this Higher anti-Semitism has now reached its climax when every discovery of recent years is called to bear witness against us and to accuse us of spiritual larceny.

Some time ago I saw in one of the numerous sheets of this country a reference to the Hammurabi Code, concluding with the words, "this means a blow to Orthodoxy." I hold no brief for Orthodoxy in this country or elsewhere. But, may I ask: Is there any wing in Judaism which is prepared to confirm the reproach of Carlyle, who, in one of his anti-Semitic fits, exclaimed, "The Jews are always dealing in old clothes; spiritual or material." We are here between ourselves, so we may frankly make the confession that we did not invent the art of printing; we did not discover America, in spite of Kayserling; we did not inaugurate the French Revolution, in spite of some one else; we were not the first to utilize the power of steam or electricity, in spite of any future Kayserling. Our great claim to the gratitude of mankind is that we gave to the world the word of God, the Bible. We have stormed heaven to snatch down this heavenly gift, as the Paitanic expression is; we threw ourselves into the breach and covered it with our bodies against every attack; we allowed ourselves to be slain by hundreds and thousands rather than become unfaithful to it; and we bore witness to its truth and watched over its purity in the face of a hostile world. The Bible is our sole *raison d'être*, and it is just this which the Higher anti-Semitism is seeking to destroy, denying all our claims for the past, and leaving u without hope for the future.

Can any section among us afford to concede to this professorial and imperial anti-Semitism and confess "for a truth we and our ancestors have sinned;" we have lived on false pretenses and were the worst shams in the world? Forget not that we live in an historical age in which everybody must show his credentials from the past. The Bible is our patent of nobility granted to us by the Almighty God, and if we disown the Bible, leaving it to the tender mercies of a Wellhausen, Stade and Duhm, and other beautiful souls working away at diminishing the "nimbus of the Chosen People," the world will disown us. There is no room in it for spiritual parvenus. But this intellectual persecution can only be fought by intellectual weapons and unless we make an effort to recover our Bible and to think out our theology for ourselves, we are irrevocably lost from both worlds. A mere protest in the pulpit or a vigorous editorial in a paper, or an amateur essay in a monthly, or even a special monograph will not help us. We have to create a really living, great literature, and do the same for the subjects of theology and the Bible that Europe has done for Jewish history and philology. It is in view of this fact that I hail Dr. Kohler's election to the Presidency of the Hebrew Union College as a happy event in the annals of American Jewry; for under his guidance I am sure Cincinnati will, in good time, contribute its share to this great "battle of duty." Some amiable persons predict jealousy and strife between the two colleges, and are already preparing to enjoy the fight as disinterested spectators. I am certain that they will prove false prophets, for the old dictum that the students of the Torah increase peace in the world, holds good also in our day. But let me say to you that this yearning after peace, on my part, is not to be taken as a sign of my entertaining any doubt as to the soundness of my theological position, or fear of a strenuous life. I am, as a rule, not given to mental squinting, nor have I ever shunned a fight. But I honor and admire Dr. Kohler too much to take up the position of an antagonist. Besides, you have probably heard the story of that Methodist parson who rebuked one of his parishioners who occasionally indulged in wife-beating, with the words: "How can you spend your time in fighting your wife, when you both should be fighting the devil?" In fact, I feel that we are standing now before a crisis which would stigmatize the indulgence in such a fight as treason to the cause of Judaism; we must gather our forces and fight the enemy; and Dr. Kohler, by his wide learning, contagious enthusiasm and noble character, is the right man in the right place to marshal a part of these forces, which may, by the blessing of God, help us to victory.

THE SEMINARY AS A WITNESS.*

JAMES Russell Lowell in one of his political essays laid down the principle that it is the duty of every great nation to produce great men. With all due deference to all sorts of mediocrities, I venture to say that the same principle is to be applied to matters spiritual, and that it is also the duty of every great religion to produce great men. In the absence of these—the great men—a nation is apt to degenerate into a mere mob governed by the petty and selfish interests of its various factions, without any vitalizing and uniting principle to sustain it on its day of peril; while religion in a similar condition is sure to dissolve into a mere series of excitements of ranting sects, without any philosophy and inspiring idea, and liable to become the prey of all sorts of quacks and flaring orators, who are certain to forsake it at the prospect of some fresh sensation, or the bidding of some new fashion. The great men are not frequent; in fact, they belong to the section of humanity of which the Rabbis have said that they are so few that the Holy One, blessed be He, distributed them over all generations so that humanity at large may profit by their counsel; as it is said (I Samuel 2:8), "For the rocks of the earth are the Lord's, and He set the world upon them."

But however rare they may be, the rocks do exist, notwithstanding all demagogic clamor which would

*Address delivered at the Dedication of the Seminary Building, April 26, 1903.

make us believe that heaven particularly favors the gravel.

Now, if we do not want to earn the opprobrium of our enemies, reproaching us with being too mechanical, the mission of seminaries should prominently consist in providing religion with great men who would prove to be its very rocks and pillars. But what are the conditions under which greatness must develop? They are many and manifold, and the time at my disposal makes it impossible to enter here into details, but with your kind permission I will say a few words on one or two of these conditions, which are of a more general character, and which seem to me to be of the utmost importance for the prosperity of our religious institutions. The first condition is the creation of a proper spiritual atmosphere.

An ancient Rabbinic tractate dealing with the methods of acquiring wisdom counts not less than forty-eight qualifications which the student should possess. But apart from the few intellectual qualifications, which are, after all, a gift of nature, they may all be summed up in the single Hebrew word, לשמה Lishmah, which means the study of the Torah for the sake of God, without an eye to any worldly advantages. "Say not," teaches the Sifre, "I will study Torah in order that I may attain the title of Rabbi or Chacham, or that I may get a salary, or that I may be rewarded for it in the world to come, but devote thyself to it for the sake of the love of God."

This is not a very practical program. Modern conditions make it necessary, I am afraid, that even our training schools for the sacred calling should be

largely conducted on the unsacred principle of the
ultimate material success of the alumni. But let us
not be too successful. For it is this consideration of
ulterior motives which is responsible for the fact
that latter day Judaism is almost entirely devoid of
the element of saintliness, without which religion
itself becomes profane and secularized.

It is very difficult to give an exact definition of
saintliness. Saintliness is the last in the scale of
the ten virtues leading up to the gift of the Holy
Spirit (*Ruach Hakodesh*), and as such it defies
analysis; but it may perhaps be dimly described as
the feminine—not feminized—element of religion,
furnishing it with the compounds of delicacy and
chasteness. It shudders at the touch of anything
sensational or vulgar; it shrinks back from all publicity, for it is "the glory of the king's daughter to
be within," not on the market place and thorough-
fares. It is unpractical and self-sacrificing, and
certainly not free from ascetic tendencies. It labors
more with the heart than with the lungs, but its very
silence is eloquent. A glance, or a nod of approval
or a sigh, not to say a tear coming from one in possession of saintliness, is with noble and sensitive souls
more effective than cartloads of volumes of finished
oratory. The title of such a saint is neither Rabbi,
nor Doctor, nor Professor, nor even Dean or President, but as our sages tell us, he is called friend,
beloved, lover of God and lover of mankind. "The
Torah," whose secrets are revealed unto him, "clothes
him with meekness and reverence. He becomes

modest, long suffering and forgiving, and it makes him great and exalts him above all things." This was the ideal scholar and saint of the old Rabbinic times, and he will certainly never appear on our globe again, as long as we do not alter the standard of greatness, and make room for him in the economy of our higher religious institutions.

In one of his philosophical works Maimonides declared that he would feel no compunction in being useful to one wise man at the risk of injuring ten thousand fools. Such a division of humanity is rather invidious, considering the largeness of the dividend and the smallness of the divisor, but I think that none of us will hesitate to employ the best means that may be helpful toward the producing of a single saint at the risk of inconveniencing crowds of theological skyscrapers and ecclesiastical office seekers.

Another condition for producing greatness is that the teaching in our seminaries should be wide and comprehensive, containing within itself the elements of eternity and catholicity. I will explain myself: Among the various legends attaching to the account of the revelation on Mount Sinai there is one to the effect that this glorious act was not only witnessed by the master of the prophets and his contemporaries, but also by those who departed from these regions long since and who came to life again for that blissful moment, as well as by the souls of those who were still to be born. "For," the Rabbis proceed to say, "was it not said by Moses, 'Neither with you only do I make this covenant and this oath, but with him that standeth here with us this day before the

Lord our God, and also with him that is not here and
with us this day.' " The underlying idea is that a
religious manifestation, to be truly great and inspiring, must also have regard for those who are not there.
It must include both an appeal to the past, to which
it should give back life and continuity, and hold out
a good message to the future, which would, in its
turn, endow it with immortality. It is true that it
is the present and its needs which have the first
claims upon our attention, and I would be sorry indeed to see the Jewish ministry proof against the
demands of our own times. What attracted me many
years ago to Krochmal's famous work was the title,
The Guide of the Perplexed of the Times, thereby
showing that every time has its own perplexities and
therefore is in need of its own guidance; but it is also
from this immortal work and other kindred works
from which I have learned that unless it is a present
which forms a link between two eternities, representing an answer of Amen to the past and an Opening Prayer to the future, it will be a very petty
present indeed, while its so-called needs will often
turn out to be a mere caprice of the mob, or a whim
of fashion, or the hobby of some wilful individual,
sure to disappear when viewed *sub specie aeternitatis*.

Perhaps I may be permitted to read here with
relation to such needs the following passage from a
book existing only in proof. After showing that
Judaism has the same powers of adaptability as
any other religion, the author proceeds to say:

"It must, however, be remarked that this satis-
fying the needs of anybody and everybody, of every

moment and every fleeting season, is not the highest ideal which Judaism set before itself. Altogether I venture to think," our author says, "that the now fashionable test of determining the worth of religion by its capability to supply the various demands of the great market of believers has something low and mercenary about it. Nothing less than a good old honest heathen Pantheon, with beautiful gods, jovial gods, lusty gods, ailing gods, fighting gods, intoxicated gods, male gods and female gods—nothing less than this would satisfy the crazes and imaginary cravings of our pampered humanity, with its pagan reminiscences, its metaphysical confusion of languages, its aesthetic pretensions, and its theological idiosyncracies. No! True religion is above all these silly demands. It is not a jack-of-all-trades, meaning Monotheism to the philosopher, Pluralism to the crowd, some mysterious Nothing to the agnostic, Pantheism to the poet, and Service of Man to the Hero worshipper. Its mission is just as much to teach the world that there are false gods and false ideals as to bring it nearer to the true one. It means to convert the world, not to convert itself. It disdains a victory by defeating itself, in giving up its essential doctrines, its most sacred symbols, its most precious traditions and its most vital teaching. It has confidence in the world; it hopes and prays and waits patiently for the Great Day when the world will be ripe for its acceptance."

And least of all will the instruction suited to the needs of such an isolated and detached present ever embody any features of greatness. "Had Dante's

scope," says a great critic, "been narrowed to contemporary Italy, the 'Divine Comedy' would have
been a picture book merely." Picture books are very
pleasant, and useful enough for babies and grown up
children, but certainly not great.

With the Bible in particular it is this feature of
eternity which is so striking even to the imagination
of those whom nobody will ever suspect of any
dogmatic bias or prejudice in favor of any particular
creed. Listen only to the following passage taken
from a book of Sir James G. Frazer, the famous
editor of *Pausanias,* and the not less famous author
of the *Golden Bough.* It reads thus:

"Apart from all questions of its religious and
historical import, which do not here concern us, the
Bible is an epic, if not a history, of the world; or, to
change the metaphor, it unrolls a vast panorama in
which the ages of the world move before us in a long
train of solemn imagery, from the creation of the
earth and the heavens onward to the final passing
away of all this material universe, and the coming of
a new heaven and a new earth wherein shall dwell
righteousness. Against this gorgeous background,
this ever shifting scenery, now bright with the hues
of heaven, now lurid with the glare of hell, we see
mankind strutting and playing their little part on
the stage of history. We see them taken from the
dust and returning to the dust; we see the rise and
fall of empires; we see great cities, now the hive of
busy multitudes, now silent and desolate, a den of
wild beasts. All life's fever is there—its loves and
hopes and joys, its high endeavors, its suffering and

sin and sorrow. And then, last scene of all, we see the Great White Throne and the endless multitude gathered before it; we hear the final doom pronounced; and as the curtain falls, we catch a glimpse of the fires of hell and the glories of heaven—a vision of the world (how different from this!) where care and sin and sorrow shall be no more, where the saints shall rest from their labors, and where God Himself shall wipe away all tears from their eyes."

Nor must the teaching in the Seminary be overmuch burdened with the considerations of locality. The Directors of this institution, by terming it the "Jewish Theological Seminary *of America*," have distinctly shown their intention of avoiding sectarianism; for it is an especial American feature that no preference is given to any denomination or sect or theological *Richtung*. They are all alike welcome, each working out its salvation in its own fashion. Again, if there is a feature in American religious life more prominent than any other, it is its conservative tendency. The history of the United States does not begin with the Red Indian, and the genesis of its spiritual life is not to be traced back to the vagaries of some peculiar sects. This country is, as everybody knows, a creation of the Bible, particularly the Old Testament, and the Bible is still holding its own, exercising enormous influence as a real spiritual power, in spite of all the destructive tendencies, mostly of foreign make. Nay, it is this very excess of zeal and the over-realization of the presence of Biblical times which unfortunately enabled quacks to create new Tabernacles here, with new Zions and Jerusalems, and to proclaim themselves as second or first Moseses, and even to profit their followers with caricature revelations. But these are only the excesses. The large bulk of the real American people have, in matters of religion, retained their sobriety and loyal adherence to the Scriptures, as their Puritan forefathers did. America thus stands both for wideness of scope and for conservatism. But be this as it may, forget not that this is a *Jewish* Theological Seminary, having the mission to teach the doctrines and the literature of the religion which is as old as history itself and as wide as the world. Any attempt to confine its activity to the borders of a single country, even be it as large as America, will only make its teachings provincial, narrow and unprofitable. Israel, and Israel alone, must be the end for which synagogues and seminaries are erected, even in this country. Thus teaches the Book of Maccabees: "God did not choose His people (Israel) for the sake of the place (that is, His Temple), but the place for the sake of the people."

I am not an opponent of state rights, and much less of the rights of a whole continent, and I readily concede that the Seminary should always give due consideration to the religious needs of this country. For instance, I am of opinion that we should in this country, with its peculiar theological atmosphere, pay more attention to Bible and theology than we did in Europe. I am further of opinion that in a democratic country like this, everything should be avoided in the teaching of theological institutions which is calculated to emphasize the difference between layman and Rabbi. I am also inclined to think that any attempt towards the centralization of the spiritual power into the hands of a man or a body of men will only prove injurious to this country, with its free and broad spirit. But these, and many other questions like these, of a disciplinary nature, are of minor importance. The great body of Jewish doctrine and Jewish law as taught by Catholic Israel has nothing in it to collide with the American spirit, and the Seminary to be really great will have to be catholic, and of a uniting nature.

There is an old Jewish prayer reading thus: "Oh, God, protect me against the day when one part (of my body) will become a burden to the other." Unfortunately, there are symptoms that this day is not far. There is even a tendency noticeable not only to hasten this day, but at last to drop the burden and to give up all notion of solidarity and of mutual responsibility. There is no other way to save us from such a calamity but to strengthen our loyalty to the Torah and to devote ourselves to its study.

Lord John Morley, in his essay on Emerson, relates that while the New England mystic was lecturing, one of the audience asked his neighbor: "Can you tell me what connection there is between that last sentence and the one that went before, and what connection it all has with Plato?" "None, my friend, save in God!" If I were asked what connection is there, say, in order to except present company, between Rabbi Moses ben Maimon, of Cordova (known as Maimonides), and Solomon ben Isaac, of Troyes (known as Rashi), I would say, "None,

save in God and His Torah." The one lived under a
Mohammedan government; the other under a Christian government. The one spoke Arabic; the other
French. The one had all the advantage of an Eastern
civilization, the other lived in the barbaric West.
The one was a merchant, afterwards a famous
physician in the great capitals of Cordova and Cairo;
the other was a Rabbi, without salary, in an unim-
portant provincial city. The one was a *persona
grata* for many years of his life at the court of Saladin,
"the most enlightened despot who ever sat on a
throne;" the other probably never had the good, or
rather the bad fortune, of ever speaking even to the
chief constable of his place. The one was a thorough
Aristotelian and possessed of all the culture of his
day; the other was an exclusively Rabbinic scholar
and hardly knew the name of Aristotle. The one
was all system and method, writing everything in
a smooth, elegant style; the other belonged to the
great inarticulates, and wrote very little beyond
commentaries and "occasional notes." But as they
both observed the same fasts and feasts; as they
both revered the same sacred symbols, though they
put different interpretations on them; as they both
prayed in the same language—Hebrew; as they both
were devoted students of the same Torah, though
they often differed in its explanation; as they both
looked back to Israel's past with admiration and
reverence, though Maimonides' conception of the
Revelation, for instance, largely varied from that of
Rashi; as their ultimate hopes centred in the same
redemption—in one word, as they studied the Torah

and lived in accordance with its laws, and both made
the hopes of the Jewish nation their own, the bonds
of unity were strong enough even to survive the
misunderstandings between their respective followers.
And they both became the rocks and pillars of
Judaism; and a Leopold Zunz, or an Isaac Hirsch
Weiss, of Vienna, were able to appreciate both Rashi
and Maimonides, and to fall in love with both of
them. It is only by strengthening these bonds of
unity, by appreciating everything Jewish and falling
in love with it, that this great monument presented
to us and to Judaism by our noble donor, whom one
dares not thank but in oblique sentences, will become
a blessing and a prayer, and, like the trans-Jordanic
altar of the Book of Joshua, it will stand not only
for unity and brotherhood, but like that, it will also
be called witness, "for it shall be a witness between
us that the Lord is God!"

SPIRITUAL HONEYMOONS.*

IN THE days of yore, when Babylon formed the
centre of Jewish civilization, and the eyes of the
whole of Israel were turned toward the banks of the
Euphrates and the Tigris for instruction and enlight-
enment, they had the goodly custom to meet twice a
year in religious convention; once at the end of the
winter, and again at the end of the summer. These
conventions, which usually met at the great seats of
learning, Sura and Pumbedita, were honored with the
presence of the heads of the Academies, the chiefs of
the Colleges, the Princes of the Captivity, and the
Judges of the Gate. These men of light and leading,
they and their disciples, and the disciples of their
disciples, all flocked there with the purpose of fighting
out the "Battle of the Torah," until every obscurity
was made clear, and every law was fixed, "citing
proof from the Bible, the Mishnah, and the Talmud,"
thus removing every stumbling-block from the path
of Israel. The session extended over a whole month,
and the days on which they met were called the "Days
of the Kallah." The term is rather obscure, but we
shall not go far wrong if, with some scholars, we render
it the "Days of the Bride," thus implying the mystical
conception of man's communion with God, in which
the Torah figures as the bride, and the act of Revelation as wedding heaven to earth. These conventions

---

*Address delivered at the Biennial Meeting of the Jewish Theo-
logical Seminary of America, March 20, 1904.

were then considered as a sort of spiritual honey-
moon. Court was paid to the Torah, and fresh
declarations of love and devotion and loyalty were
made to her.

But times have changed and we have changed with
the times. We have grown too old and too sober for
semi-annual honeymoons. Life is too strenuous, and
the demands upon the time of our communal workers
are too great to allow any hope of such protracted
meetings of a month's duration. We must, therefore,
be satisfied with biennial conventions, and it gives me
much pleasure to welcome you here, in the Jewish
Theological Seminary of America, as the President of
the Institution, and to thank you for the support you
have granted us.

At a biennial convention, held many years ago,
the late Dr. Sabato Morais, the founder of this
institution, expressed himself to the following effect:

"If my voice could but reach many a wealthy man
in the city of New York, I would picture to them
ancestral Judaism in the act of imploring that it may
not be suffered to perish; Judaism entreating for the
means that will nurture and raise spiritual physicians,
Rabbis skilled in the art of infusing into our religious
body fresher and more vigorous powers."

The righteous are greater in their death than in
their life, and their supplications have reached not
only the wealthiest, but at the same time some of the
noblest and best among us, who hastened to come to
the relief of this institution, and established it on a
firm basis. It is no exaggeration to say that no Jewish
seminary, either in this country or abroad, can lay

claim to be better equipped than we are. Our Seminary is located in a building most suitable for its purpose; it commands a staff of teachers, the majority of whom may be called thorough specialists in their subjects; it has a large number of pupils; it is in possession of a library, collected and donated by Judge Sulzberger with the best of judgment and with the greatest of sacrifices, such as no other seminary in the world can show. Writing lately on certain Halachic portions of the Sifre, very complicated and hard to understand, I had the satisfaction to find in the Judge's collection not less than five commentaries on the book mentioned, greatly helping me to clear up a very obscure subject; whilst till now, when under similar difficulties, I could only appeal to one commentary at my disposal. This is a fact which every one of us will appreciate at once.

I have spoken of the "Battles of the Torah" that were waged in the ancient semi-annual conventions. The shortness of our meeting does not allow me to invite you to join here in these battles. They must be fought out by the Faculty and the students—I hope not between the Faculty and the students—but you will be interested to learn that we still adhere to the old custom of "citing proof from the Bible, and the Mishnah and the Talmud." These in all their ramifications are the subjects which are taught here.

Bible occupies a prominent place in our curriculum, and I am happy to say that it is taught by a man of a thorough university training, who occupied the position of Privatdocent in one of the great German universities. The subject is thus taught in agreement

with the best critical methods. Provision has also
been made for a course of lectures introductory to
the Bible, in which the views about the rise and
development of the canon, both of the ancient and of
the modern schools, will be expounded to the classes.
Our reason for deferring this course of lectures to a
later stage in the schedule is that we find it advisable
that our pupils should first know something *of* the
Bible before they learn everything *about* the Bible.
But I must tell you distinctly that with all the
allowance we are making for Bible criticism and
modern requirement, we are not prepared to reconstruct the Bible in accordance with every whim of the
latest commentator. If I have any hope for myself
and for those who are to be trained in this institution, it is that the Bible will reconstruct us.

When a certain student approached Maimonides
some eight hundred years ago with a rather difficult
question, relating to the fall of man as narrated in the
third chapter of Genesis, the beginning of Maimonides' answer was: "You appear to have studied the
matter superficially, and imagine that you can understand a book which has been the guide of past and
present generations, when you for a moment with-
draw from your lusts and appetites, and glance over
its contents as if you were reading a story or some
poetical composition. Collect your thoughts and
examine the matter carefully, for it is not to be understood as you first thought, but as you will find after
due deliberation." In this blessed century of ours,
when men who have hardly mastered the vocabulary
of the Hebrew language parade as infallible critics,

I can only add to Maimonides' advice: Learn a little more Hebrew, study a little more the text and less commentaries and introductions, make yourself thoroughly acquainted with its idioms and the methods of composition in ancient Israel, and you will find "after due deliberation that the matter is not to be understood as you first thought."

The same critical methods are pursued in our teaching of Rabbinic literature, which, besides the Talmud Babli, also includes the Talmud of Jerusalem and the ancient Tannaitic Midrashim, as the Torat Kohanim, the Mechilta, the Sifre, and the other ancient Rabbinic collections, without which a scientific study of the old Rabbinic literature is impossible.

On a closer examination of these works you will find that large portions of them consist of Halachah. The term Halachah is variously translated. Those who have never given a thought to it render it casuistry, and are proud of their ignorance; whilst to those who have studied it, the Halachah represents the legal portion of Jewish literature accompanied by argument, and they endeavor to increase their knowledge of it. Now, there was a good deal of comment lately in the press as to the advisability of the study of the Halachah for the Occidental man, and I owe you some explanation for our alloting so much time to it. But can any one tell men exactly where the Occidental man is to be found? I read in a paper the other day that it is only Kansas which can lay claim to pure Occidentalism, and that Chicago itself is Orientalized. If it is a matter of geography, I think that the State of Washington or the Territory of Alaska are the only regions which can claim this honor; but if it is a question of intellect and learning, I will mention the great Occidental man who died lately, considered the greatest historian, and known on both sides of the Atlantic. I refer to Professor Mommsen. It was this Mommsen who wrote the famous history of the Roman Empire, but at the same time published many volumes on the jurisprudence of the Romans, and as many volumes again on inscriptions dating from antiquity. To mention another Occidental man, I will name Gibbon, the greatest historian the English race has ever produced, whose work *The Decline and Fall of the Roman Empire*, has passed through the furnace of nineteenth century criticism without becoming antiquated; but a full account of the Halachah of the Romans is incorporated in his great history, as may be seen from the forty-fourth chapter of his work, which passes as one of the best digests of the Roman law. As to our constitutional historians, they do not draw all their knowledge of your past from the prayers which traveling ministers deliver on occasion at Congress, or from the addresses of Congressional chaplains. As far as I know, their statements are largely based on the study of the English codes, your own collection of Revised Statutes and the decisions of the Supreme Court. Of Jewish historians, I will mention here Leopold Herzfeld, whose *Geschichte des Volkes Jisrael von Vollendung des Zweiten Tempels bis zur Einsetzung des Mackabaers Schimon* forms the most critical and most thorough piece of history ever written by a Jew. He was one of our best Halachists,

and his work is especially distinguished by the painstaking care with which the author studied the legal
portions of Rabbinic literature, and the scientific
method in which he utilized them.

As every one knows who has occupied himself
with the study of Jewish history, the greatest defects
of many works in this field are due to the fact that
their authors were largely ignorant of the Halachah
and lacking in a real appreciation of Jewish mysticism. They have thus missed the central springs
both of Jewish reason and of Jewish emotion.

I by no means entertain the hope that all our
Rabbis will develop into Mommsens or even Herz-
felds, but I consider it important for the honor of
America, and of American Israel in particular, that
our institutions of learning should be conducted on
such lines as not to exclude all possibility of presenting the world one day with a great scholar and a
deep thinker.

In addition to these subjects, we have also regular
lectures on Jewish history, Jewish theology, Jewish
philosophy, Jewish archaeology and Jewish liturgy.
Hellenistic literature and the Apocryphal Books have
also their share. We also insist that the student who
comes to us should be in possession of a B. A. degree
or some equivalent to it, bearing evidence to his classical training. We consider this as most essential for
the equipment of a Rabbi. The Rabbi should be
"the greatest of his brethren," and there must be no
department of human thought in which he should
stand as inferior to any member of his congregation
who has enjoyed a liberal education. But apart from

this consideration, I am certain that such a training will prove most helpful to develop the conservative tendencies of our young men and will give them that gravity, without which the public speaker becomes a mere windbag and ranter. We should never have witnessed these wild excesses in our pulpits and platforms, had our orators, who talk so much of individuality and individualism, gone through a proper course of Greek and Latin classics. They would have had a better understanding of what humanity now owes to antiquity and to its past, and would have been less confident of their power to turn the wheel of history. Of course, Greek and Latin are no guarantee against skepticism, but my experience has been that what the thoroughly educated man doubted first and last was *his* own infallibility. We consider it also important that the Rabbi should have a wide acquaintance with the masterpieces of English literature, both in prose and verse. Their study will give a chasteness to the style of the student, and make him the enemy of all forms of blatant superficiality. He will learn from them that thoroughness is a part of excellence, and that self-complacency is the companion of ignorance. More than this, he will come to feel a wholesome diffidence as to his own knowledge and his own powers, and will regard only the most mature thought and careful presentation as becoming his office and as worthy of acceptance.

You will say probably that this is rather an elaborate process for training ministers. I admit it. But don't forget the age of elixirs and universal remedies has passed away. There was a time when the "blessed" words, "Israel's Mission," "Evolution," and "Progress" were powerful enough to make the fortunes of a preacher for the whole of his life if he possessed the necessary shouting organs to give them sufficient emphasis and accentuation. Alas! Times have changed, and these universal remedies have lost their virtue with us. Serious-minded men suddenly made the discovery that the missionaries came so close to being converted themselves that it was almost impossible to discern between the teacher and those who were meant to become the novices. Again, some of those who know best the meaning of the word "Evolution" doubt greatly its applicability to ethics and to matters spiritual. Personally, when I hear how some of our youngsters solemnly declare to their congregations that the modern minister is a three-fold being, composed of Rabbi, preacher and prophet, and that he may choose soon to reveal himself in this last capacity—I say, when I hear such announcements and think of Israel's great seers in bygone times— I can only wish that the process of evolution might have stopped at Isaiah and Habbakuk. As to "Progress," the question is where shall we progress? When one, in his forward movements, has reached an abyss where one step more would mean death and ruin, he will instinctively shrink back and retrace his steps. The only difference is that those who possess the moral courage, turn their faces from the abyss and walk in the direction from which they have started; whilst the others, like the dead in the myth, unable to avert their eyes from the place of their

former attractions, walk backwards. But back they
go all the same, in spite of all their professions of
"Progress." Judaism cannot be dismissed with a few
general meaningless phrases. Judaism is, as I have
often insisted upon, and shall insist upon again on
every public occasion, a positive religion, with a
Sacred Writ and a continuous tradition. It is a
discipline of life and has a philosophy of its own. It
has distinct precepts, and usages, and customs,
consecrated by the consent of Catholic Israel through
thousands of years, and hallowed by the agony and
the tears of the martyrs. It has a wide literature
running through all historic ages, with numberless
junctions branching off into every department of
human thought. It has one of the most ancient
liturgies of the world, of constant growth and development, but still remaining intact in its main features.
The knowledge of such a religion can be acquired only
by serious study and elaborate training, which must
necessarily last for years.

But there is also another point which I should like
to submit to your consideration, and in which your
co-operation is urgently needed. Oliver Wendell
Holmes once remarked:

"These United States furnish the greatest market
for intellectual *green fruit* of all the places in the
world. The demand for intellectual labor is so enormous and the market so far from nice that young
talent is apt to fare like unripe gooseberries—get
plucked to make a fool of."

We are trying our best to improve the market and
to make it "nice." But it is also necessary that you

on your part should be more careful in your demand; that you should allow young talent to ripen. This is not merely a question of finances, but it is a question of raising the standard of the qualification of the ministry altogether. Study requires ripening, and the problems of Judaism are not such that a young man of twenty might master them, even if he were a genius. All our labors will be in vain as long as those who have hardly begun to learn are burdened with the office of teaching. The pioneer season, with its partial savagery, its unrest, its haste, and its adventurous character, has given way to settled, solid and methodical habits of life, and it is high time that the Synagogue should come to its rights, and be dealt with in the same careful and solemn manner as is accorded to all other higher interests of the community. It is only then that Judaism will be able to re-discover itself, and to accomplish those sacred duties for which our ancestors died, and for which we hope to live.

REBELLION AGAINST BEING A PROBLEM.*

OF ALL the various banquets and receptions given in honor of great men which it has ever been my privilege to attend, none has afforded me more gratification than the opportunity offered to me of being present at this dinner, given in honor of our revered guest, Monsieur Anatole Leroy-Beaulieu, Member of the Institute of France. For thus said Rabbi Abin, who apparently plagiarized Carlyle some fifteen centuries before the Scotch seer wrote his "Heroes and Hero Worship:" "He who sits at the festive board at which the true sage and scholar is entertained, enjoys a foretaste of that bliss which man experiences by direct communion with the Divine." It is in such moments of grace that genius relaxes into geniality, and elaborate learning expands into wit and *esprit*, and deep thought takes the shape of that delightful and profitable proverbial wisdom which has created our "table-talk literature," and of which the speeches just delivered have given you such a fine specimen.

The sense of gratification is increased by the feeling of gratitude which we all harbor towards the author of *Israel Among the Nations*. As a native of Roumania, I feel under an especial debt of gratitude towards our distinguished guest. The troubles of the Roumanian Jew begin with perceiving the light of

---

*Address delivered at Banquet in honor of the late Anatole Leroy-Beaulieu, May 16, 1904.

the world. On the very day on which he receives his
name, by which he is called up to the Torah in later
life, he loses his çivil and political rights, and becomes
subject to all sorts of restrictive laws. On the occasion of my first fight with the boys of our Christian
neighbors, I was warned not to hit back, as such a
presumption on my part may bring serious misfortune
upon the whole of the Jewish community. On
remonstrating that it is unfair that the Christian
boys should enjoy all immunity in their fights, I was
given to understand that we belonged to a people
which is under the curse of being a problem, and that
I must wait for an answer until the Jewish problem
has found its proper solution. Naturally, I rebelled
against being a problem, and I pondered a great deal
over its meaning. I was perhaps a boy of twelve
or fourteen when there fell into my hands a Hebrew
translation of Josephus' *Contra Apion*, which I read
with great interest, though it was only partially
understood by me, and I well remember that I wondered whether our Christian neighbors had ever read
"Apion," and whether this might not be the cause of
their ill-will against us. I must say to their honor
that they were not addicted to the reading of books,
and that they were quite original in their hatred and
Jew-baiting, but those were still the days when
French influence was predominant on the shores of
the Danube. When matters assumed dangerous
proportions, there used to come messages from the
West, echoing the voice of God and humanity as
revealed unto His servants who inaugurated the
French Revolution, which made our neighbors under-

stand that there is still a Providence in the world
watching even over the destiny of the Jew.

With the year 1870, the reign of blood and iron
began. Humanity was gradually deposed. A new
generation arose which knew not the traditions of
the French Revolution and the "fifth-beast of Daniel"
was let loose. Hatred and malice and envy and brutality of the worst kind were set free against a de-
fenseless people. But what was worse, was that all
these brutal instincts, till then held at bay by reason
of public opinion, were raised to the dignity of an
"ism," and the term "Anti-Semitism" was invented.
The Jewish problem became more complicated
every day, and a large literature was created. Instead of being a mere religious problem, we suddenly
discovered ourselves to be also an ethnological problem, an economic problem, a social problem, a psycho-
logical problem, and ever so many more problems.
I need hardly describe to you under what torture
the Jew is when wading through this degraded and
degrading literature. It is actual vivisection, without
the relief of anaesthetics. Some Mohammedan theologians are said to have seriously discussed whether
women have a soul. These anti-Semitic scribblers
took it for granted that we have no soul, no sense
of honor, no feelings of dignity, and were quite
astonished when we showed signs of resentment.

You may then realize what a relief it was to come
upon the work *Israel Among the Nations*. It is a
noble book. It is written in a thoroughly scientific
spirit. It is not the Jew who constitutes the problem
for the author. It is rather the phenomenon that the

Jew was made to constitute a problem in the nineteenth century.   Just as a scientific investigator
examines into the causes of an epidemic, our author
subjects to an analysis the symptoms of the spiritual
malady that has afflicted humanity.   Jew and
Christian alike are arraigned before his tribunal.
The Jews do not escape censure.   Indeed we are
not faultless. We raise no claim to perfection. But
one always has the feeling that "those are the wounds
inflicted by a friend."   In Jewish angelology, the
Angel Michael figures as "An Angel of Letters,"
or as they expressed it, the Prince of Wisdom, but
he is described at the same time as the friend and the
advocate of Israel.   The savant Leroy-Beaulieu is
a great man of letters in the best and the widest
sense of the word, but what he accomplished as an
advocate of Israel, he has shown in the book just
named.   He not only attempts to reconcile us with
the rest of the world, but also with ourselves, or with
that section of the Jewish community which forms
our particular problem.   It is a Prince of Wisdom
who offers us this wise counsel with regards to
our problem:

"Some of the Jewish emigrants," he says, "have
been obviously degraded and corrupted by centuries
of oppression.   Many years—perhaps one or two
generations—will be needed to raise their moral
plane, to imbue them with a sense of honor and
dignity.   It is a great mistake to believe that this
moral uplifting can be facilitated by detaching them
from their religion. On the contrary, the least praise-
worthy Jews that I have met have generally been

'de-judaised' Jews, those who had ceased to observe the Mosaic law."

As a student of Jewish literature, it was only natural that I should be eager to learn the opinion of this great man of letters on the various productions of Jewish genius. An after-dinner speech is not a fit occasion to enter into a learned discourse. But one general remark will not be out of place. My perusal of *Israel Among the Nations* impressed me as if M. Leroy-Beaulieu, who is himself a pious Christian, feels some anxiety about the fate of the Old Testament, under these attacks by the "higher" and "lower" anti-Semitism. To his comfort, and to the comfort of all gathered here, let me say that I am very hopeful in this respect. Perhaps I may reproduce here the following story from the Reverend Edward Everett Hale's book, "Lowell and His Friends:"

"I am not sure," our late Senatorial Chaplain says, "that this story of those days is quite decorous enough for print. But I will risk it. Professor Calvin Ellis Stowe, who was a classmate of Long-fellow's, told me that in the early days of '61, he met Longfellow in the streets of Boston. Both of them were in haste, but Longfellow had time enough to ask if the Andover gentlemen were all alive to their duty to the nation. Stowe said he thought they were, and Longfellow said, 'If the New Testament won't do, you must give them the Old.' "

This is not said in disparagement of the New Testament. All that I desire to suggest is that the Old Testament is an elemental force of morality which humanity may neglect for a while, but with which it cannot dispense for any length of time. We shall never cease to profit by the Old Testament as long as there exists a sense of duty, and we shall return to it whenever the need of the Divine Imperative will be felt deepest. As to the later developments of Hebrew literature, we must not forget that very little is known of it. We must recollect that the knowledge of Post-Biblical Hebrew literature is still in its infancy. The magnificent work *Les Rabbins Francais*, which we owe to the French nation, has revealed only a small part of it. Jewish literature is eminently a religious literature with a Golden Legend of its own, and a continuous record of the experience and struggles of beautiful souls. But unfortunately most of these litterateurs who have made it their main occupation in life to acquaint the world with this literature and the men who have created it, have not yet outgrown their rationalistic stage. Being mainly devoted to what I may call a *bourgeois* gospel or a *bourgeois* Torah and a Philistine conception of the universe, they were lacking in sympathy and depth of religious feeling, and devoid of all appreciation of mysticism and those qualities which make for saintliness and holiness. What I always admired in Renan was not so much his *Life of Jesus*, which is, indeed, largely antiquated now, or his *History of the People of Israel*, in which one, after having studied the works of Graf, Wellhausen, Kuenen, Stade and other "fathers of the holy church of higher criticism," finds little that is entirely new and original—what I admired most in him was his essay on Francis of Assisi, where he showed himself a master in the art of religion, and proved that his liberal tendencies have not obscured his judgment upon saints and saintliness, though he saw the weak points both in their character and in their logic. We have the saints, but we are still lacking in Renans.

Another hint offered us for our guidance by our learned author is contained in the following passage. After paying us the compliment that we are a "prophetic people," M. Leroy-Beaulieu says, "Were the Jew and the Christian equally faithful—the one to the Gospel and the other to the Torah—the points of difference between them would be fewer than those of resemblance." These are fair stipulations to which all, both Jews and Christians, could subscribe with a good conscience, and it is for a reconciliation on such terms of loyalty to our pasts and devotion to our religions that peace is desirable. An American writer, whose name escapes me, records the following pleasantry from Colonial times.

"A youth among the Friends wished to espouse a fair Puritan maiden; but the Quakers disapproved his marrying out of their society, and the Congregationalists his marrying into theirs; so in despair he thus addressed her: 'Ruth, let us break from this unreasonable bondage. I will give up my religion, and thou shalt give up thine; and we will marry and go into the Church of England, and go to the devil together!'"

I hope that both Ruth and her sweetheart are in some parlor in Heaven. There are many mansions in the House of our Father, but I tell you frankly

that I desire no bond of unity on the condition of
our going to the devil, either Jew or Christian. The
terms of M. Leroy-Beaulieu are such that we all go
to Heaven, where we shall meet him. But there is
no hurry for such a meeting. This can wait "bis
ueber hundert und zwanzig jahr, zu gesund," as the
Jewish expression is—and so let us all raise our glasses
and drink to the happiness of the author of "ISRAEL
AMONG THE NATIONS."

THE RECONCILIATION OF ISRAEL.*

THE occasion for which we have gathered today in these academic precincts, is a most solemn one. It forms an epoch both in the history of the reorganized Seminary, and in the life of those to whom I have just handed these Rabbinical diplomas. Two years are a short period—indeed too short—in the history of an institution. But it must be pointed out that the gentlemen who graduated today had pursued their theological studies under the guidance of competent teachers before the reorganization of the Seminary took place, some here, and some elsewhere, and it is only in view of this fact that my colleagues and myself felt able to grant them these diplomas. But we may say with the Scriptures, "God has done graciously with me, for I have all—all of which an Institution of learning could wish for: a splendid building, a great library, an excellent teaching staff, and largely attended classes." We had in these two years experience enough to justify us in the policy which the Seminary has pursued from its very beginning; and that is, that its mission is to stand for Jewish life and Jewish thought. I have so often enlarged upon the meaning of these two terms that it is not necessary to enter into any comment upon them. In my Inaugural Address I have explained the meaning of these terms, and I

*Address delivered at the first Graduating Exercises of the Jewish Theological Seminary of America, June 5, 1904.

shall not dwell upon them to-day. I may remark, however, that our experiment to confine the teaching in the Seminary to post-graduates, that is, men who have taken their B. A. degree, did not prove such a failure as some prophesied. It is true, that not a week, I may say, has passed in the life of this Seminary in which I was not compelled to refuse admission to applicants unable to comply with our entrance requirements. But there is no help for this. We must insist that our institution be conducted on a scientific basis. There is no way of training men in any department of scholarship conducted in a scientific and methodical way without preliminary preparation afforded by such studies as are commonly included under the term of "a liberal education."

It is only by proceeding on the lines mapped out for us by Zunz, Krochmal, Rappaport, Frankel, and others, that traditional Judaism, built up on the broad basis of science and history, can ever hope to become a force and to bring about that reconciliation among the parties to which every well-wisher of Israel is looking forward.

We consider it also important that the Rabbi should have a wide acquaintance with the masterpieces of English literature, both in prose and in verse. This is the only means of understanding and making ourselves understood by our fellow-countrymen. And the Rabbi, as a representative of the community, should always prove the best means of bringing about this mutual understanding.

This brings me to the real subject of my address to-day, which is to give a few words of advice to those

who are about to enter upon their sacred callings as
Rabbis in Jewish communities. It is recorded in
ancient Jewish literature that when the congregation
delegated the man to step before the Ark and to
perform the service, they did not say unto him,
"Come and pray," but, "Deliver our battles; accomplish our reconciliation." Delivering battles and
accomplishing reconciliation was the mission of the
spiritual representatives of Israel in olden times, and
this should be your mission, my friends, when you
step before the Ark. That "Life means War," is an
old adage, but you find the spiritual life to be no less
so. In your capacity as pastors you will have to wage
war against many an evil, rampant in large cities,
the battles against which should be inspired by the
words of the minister. I say "inspired" advisedly,
as I do not think it altogether fitting that the Rabbi
should engage in the office of the public agitator or
moral detective. "You cannot," it is an old saying,
"perform the part of the broom without getting
soiled at the same time;" and the Rabbi should be
above every taint and impurity. You will have to
deliver battles against what the old Jews called the
"Mekatreg" (the Perennial Accuser), or what we would
call the savage instincts of hatred and jealousy,
which, under various disguises and under all sorts of
pretentious titles, rise against us in every generation.
Some ancient Jewish teacher maintained that Israel,
in the course of its life as a nation, has only enjoyed
one day of peace. This is indeed a bold statement.
But I may say without being guilty of exaggeration
that anybody who watched the literary productions

in the fields of history, philosophy and theology which appeared during the last generation, will find that there is seldom a book in which we are left entirely at peace, and which does not contain some charge against Israel or his religion in one shape or another. You, as the scholars of the community, will meet with the same experience, and it will be your duty to defend Israel against these unjust attacks. You will also have to hold up principles which by the very fact of their catholic spirit and their aiming at reconciliation may easily become the subject of attack by extreme parties. With regard to this latter, I in no way wish you to constitute yourselves into a sort of *Synagoga Militans*, and to widen the gap which is already deep enough to divide Israel into regular sects. The rule of action in such cases is: do your duty, state your principles clearly, and for the rest, remember the Talmudical saying, "Silence of a Babylonian testifies to his noble descent." This is the only way to accomplish reconciliation.

But chief among those you will have to fight will be your own selves. R. Bachya ben Pakudah gave us the wise counsel: "If you want to praise, praise God; if you want to blame, blame yourself." I am afraid that we do not always follow this counsel. The Midrash tells us that when Elijah said, "I have been very jealous for the Lord of Hosts that the children of Israel have forsaken Thy covenant," God said unto him, "Well, this is My covenant, not thine." The prophet then continued to say, "They have thrown down Thy altars, and slain Thy prophets with the sword." Whereupon God said unto him,

"These are My altars and My prophets: What does it concern thee?" At last Elijah said, "And I, even I only am left, and they seek my life to take it away from me." The rejoinder was, "Let the mouth which denounces Israel be crushed." Thereupon he was removed from the office of prophecy, which was transferred to Elishah, the son of Shaphat. Of course, there was no tradition about this dialogue between God and Elijah. What the Rabbis meant to convey by this paraphrase of I Kings, 19 : 10 was, that leaders representing spiritual institutions, great as they may be, are but rarely free from a certain taint of selfishness. They are thus tempted to confuse the cause for which they stand with their own selves, or even to place their selves above the cause. The temptation is the greater and the easier to satisfy among us who are still in need of an established tradition and wanting in a general public opinion in matters spiritual. Under such conditions, the leader is sometimes apt to consider his own person as the source of all authority, and to act on the principle, *"Le Judaisme c'est moi"* (I am Judaism).

My friends, beware of such a mistake, and wage war against yourself when such temptations come upon you. Neither you, nor I, nor even your Presidents or Parnassim to come, are Judaism. It is not your covenant, and they are not your prophets. We are all only humble servants of Judaism. In the narrative of Moses' first call we read, "And God said moreover unto Moses, thus shalt thou say unto the children of Israel: the Lord God of your fathers, the God of Abraham, the God of Isaac, and the God

of Jacob hath sent me unto you." (Exod. 3:15.)
Let this Scriptural verse serve as a test to you whether
you preach Judaism or yourselves. When your message is not any longer addressed to the children of
Israel, or when you cannot any longer say with a
good conscience that it is the God of your fathers
who sent you—in other words, when you have arrived
at the conviction necessitating your breach with the
Past, and compelling you to confess that the Present
is only to form a preamble to a Future Universalism,
with the consequent final absorption and extinction
of the children of Israel—then be sure that you will
not accomplish our reconciliation, and that honesty
and uprightness impose silence upon you, for you
have no message any longer.

It is further indispensable that your message shall
be clear and concise. But you will never obtain
this readiness unless you follow the rule laid down
by the Rabbis, "Let thy spirit not be so overbearing
as to venture to say anything in public before thou
hast thought over the matter between thee and thyself three or four times." You have never given me
occasion to think that you will fail in your duty by
overbearance; but there is sometimes a tendency
among young men to rely too much upon the spiritual
dowry they bring with them from their Alma Mater.
This is bad economy, and leads to intellectual bank-
ruptcy. To succeed in becoming life-long teachers, as
every minister is bound to be, you must agree to
become at the same time life-long learners. "How
came it about," we read in the Sifre, "that Israel
has become petty and dull-brained? Because they

were not building up in the words of the. Torah."
Universities and seminaries can only impress you with
the immensity of the task before you, and make you
feel the shortcomings of your attainments, and supply
you with the basis of your building. But as soon as
the foundations are laid, it is for you to complete
the work which the Seminary has begun. And unless
you are satisfied to remain small and mediocre—not to
use the harsher term of the Sifre—you should all your
life "be fixing seasons for the study of the Torah."

On this occasion allow me to also call your attention to another point which is very much at my heart.
You are all young men, and it may easily happen
that the one or the other among you will be elected
as an assisting or associate minister of an older
Rabbi. I have noted with sorrow that such positions
are very seldom productive of the desired happiness
to the parties concerned. The young minister,
coming fresh from college, brimful of life, and seeking
for an outlet for his energies, is, I fear, not always
inclined to treat his colleague with the consideration
due to him. He looks upon him as one who has already passed the "dead line," as the expression is,
and whose advice can be ignored without any det-
riment to the congregation. My friends, God pays
"measure for measure," and to such a one the punishment will be that he will grow old one day himself
and will learn that zeal and enthusiasm are only of
value when they are balanced by experience and
sound judgment, only to be acquired by mature age
and after many a bitter disappointment. One must
never forget the injunction of the Scriptures. "Thou

shalt rise up before the hoary head, and honor the
face of the old man, and fear thy God: I am the Lord."
You all know the term "B'nai Torah," "The children
of the Torah," as applied to the students of the Law,
but you will please Mother Torah best if you treat
your older brothers with brotherly love. And now,
let me hope that you will always remain faithful children both to Mother Torah and to this Alma Mater.

If I have any further wish to express, it is that this
Alma Mater which has introduced you to Mother
Torah will maintain a permanent place in your affec-
tions, and that you will give us proofs of your devotion to this institution, and loyalty to the principles
we have attempted to inculcate, as often as the
occasion may rise, and you may be sure that these
relations of devotion and loyalty will be mutual.
We shall always watch your career with interest,
and shall always be ready to be as helpful to you as
we can, and let our combined efforts be of such a
nature that we can say, "From you and me (or rather,
the institution which I have the honor to represent)
will ascend praise to the Most High."

ALTAR BUILDING IN AMERICA.*

IN THE weekly lesson read yesterday in the synagogue, both Israel's hopes and Israel's fears find supreme expression. From these chapters we will select for our meditation today the following introductory verses from the twenty-seventh chapter of Deuteronomy:

"1. And Moses with the elders of Israel commanded the people, saying, Keep all the commandments which I command you this day.

* * * * * * * * *

"4. Therefore, it shall be when ye be gone over Jordan, that ye shall set up these stones, which I command you this day, in mount Ebal, and thou shalt plaister them with plaister.

"5. And there shalt thou build an altar unto the Lord thy God, an altar of stones; thou shalt not lift up any iron tool upon them.

"6. Thou shalt build the altar of the Lord thy God of whole stones; and thou shalt offer burnt offerings thereon to the Lord thy God.

"7. And thou shalt offer peace offerings, and shalt eat there, and rejoice before the Lord thy God.

"8. And thou shalt write upon the stones all the words of this Torah very plainly." (Deut. 27:1-8.)

---

*Address delivered at the consecration of the reconstructed Synagogue of Congregation Agudath Jeshurun, Indianapolis, Ind., and the Installation of the first graduate of the Jewish Theological Seminary of America, Rabbi Charles I. Hoffman, August 28, 1904.

The building of an altar for the purpose of worship was thus a sacred duty incumbent upon Israel the moment they had come to "the rest and the inheritance," as the Holy Land is called in the Bible.

And Israel remained conscious of the fact of the imperativeness of this duty throughout the whole course of its long and checkered history. Wheresoever the Jew, the eternal wanderer, found rest, though not always an inheritance, there an altar was erected, dedicated to the worship of the Lord, the God of Israel. Thus, as far back as a thousand years ago when the dispersion of Israel covered a much smaller area than at the present day, an ancient Jewish teacher could with justice apply the Psalmist's words: "Their line is gone out through all the earth, and their words to the end of the world," to the synagogues and the Houses of Interpretation in which the Law of God was taught to the people. Our own times where the dispersion of Israel extends to the remotest corners of the earth, more and more vindicate the interpretation of this sage. If the synagogues and Houses of Interpretation were marked on the map, they would be found as universal and world encircling as mountain and river, everywhere lending color, individuality and life to our globe. Verily, "From the rising of the sun to the going down thereof, the Lord's name is praised."

Israel in America has particularly distinguished itself in this holy work of altar-building. The Talmud speaks of certain commandments which Israel received in joy, and at all times joyfully fulfilled. Considering the comparatively short period since

this country of ours was opened to civilization, the
number of places of worship erected under these
skies by both Jew and Christian proves altar building
to be an especial and favorite duty of the American
people, received in joy from the very beginning, and
to this day joyfully continued. I have heard of a
famous Jewish scholar in Europe who in his vacation,
would retire to the most isolated nooks of the Car-
pathians or ascend the loftiest summits of the Alps,
there to perform his devotions and thus hallow a
new spot on earth to the service of Almighty God.
Similar feelings must evidently have animated the
American people in their unprecedented spiritual
annexations.

The first settlers in this country were mostly men
who had left their native land for conscience' sake,
despairing of the Old World as given over to the
powers of darkness, despotism and unbelief. And I
can quite realize how they must have gloried in the
idea of being chosen instruments of Providence who
were to restore the spiritual equilibrium of the world
by the conquest of new spheres of religious influence
and their dedication to the worship of Almighty God.

As a Jew coming from the East of Europe, where
my people are trodden down, where seats of Jewish
learning and Jewish piety are daily destroyed, I am
greatly animated by the same feelings and am com-
forted to see the New World compensating us for
our many losses in the Old. I rejoice, therefore, at
the privilege of being with you on this solemn occasion. The words of the benediction, "Blessed art
Thou, O Lord our God, King of the universe, who

hath kept us in life and hath preserved us and enabled
us to reach this season," rise to my lips, and with
the consent of the Omnipresent and with the consent
of this holy congregation I declare this building
"Holiness to the Lord!"

We are now prepared for the minuter consideration of our text.

"And thou shalt write upon the stones all the
words of the Torah very plainly." The stones are
erected, and at this moment have been dedicated to
the service of God. But bricks and mortar, marble
pillar and gilded domes do not make an altar. What
constitutes an altar are the words of the Torah,
which are engraved on the very stones, which influence
the lives of the worshipers and convert their homes
into places of worship. The verse in Exodus 20:24,
also containing injunctions regarding the altar, is
paraphrased by the great Hillel as if God were saying
to man, "If thou wilt come unto My house, I will
come into thy house." "The word of our Lord
endureth forever." This is a divine promise. But
if after frequent visits to places of worship, you have
experienced nothing of the nearness of God in your
houses, then you may safely doubt whether you have
really been in a house of God. It is the home which
is the final and supreme test of the altar. A synagogue, for instance, that teaches a Judaism which
finds no reverberating echo in the Jewish home, awak-
ens there no distinctive conscious Jewish life, has
failed in its mission, and is sure sooner or later to
disappear as a religious factor making for righteousness and holiness. It may serve as a lecture hall or

a lyceum, or as a place to which people in their *ennui* repair for "an intellectual treat;" but it will never become a place of worship, a real altar for acceptable sacrifices, bestowing that element of joy in God, the *Simhah shel mizwah* of our Rabbis, which is the secret and strength of Judaism.

This is a test applicable to all ages and to all countries; to the New World as well as the Old. There is nothing in American citizenship which is incompatible with our observing the dietary laws, our sanctifying the Sabbath, our fixing a Mezuzah on our doorposts, our refraining from unleavened bread on Passover, or our perpetuating any other law essential to the preservation of Judaism. On the other hand, it is now generally recognized by the leading thinkers that the institutions and observances of religion are part of its nature, a fact that the moribund rationalism of a half century ago failed to realize. In certain parts of Europe every step in our civil and social emancipation demanded from us a corresponding sacrifice of a portion of the glorious heritage bequeathed to us by our fathers. Jews in America, thank God, are no longer haunted by such fears. We live in a commonwealth in which by the blessing of God and the wisdom of the Fathers of the Constitution, each man abiding by its laws, has the inalienable right of living in accordance with the dictates of his own conscience. In this great, glorious and free country we Jews need not sacrifice a single iota of our Torah; and, in the enjoyment of absolute equality with our fellow citizens we can live to carry out those ideals for which our ancestors so often had to die.

Another criterion of the true altar, according to our Rabbis, is that its mission is peace, Shalom.

The main function of Shalom consists, as a great Jewish-Spanish thinker teaches, in creating harmony and unity in all manifestations of life, so that every discordant note, either in action or in thought, is made impossible. "The ways of the Torah are ways of pleasantness, and all its paths are peace" (Shalom), and none of these ways, traversing all the relations of man, both to his Maker and to his fellow men, can be neglected without injury to body and soul. Thus a Jew, who is most particular in the fulfilment of the ritual laws, but is less observant of the portions of the Torah commonly described as ethical and moral, is certainly a disturber of the peace of the King of Kings, and has committed an offense for which, as you know, Heaven has renounced the prerogative of granting pardons, unless full redress is first made. And his offence is the greater as the discordant note will have a jarring effect on all the community, causing dismay and resentment in every quarter, for which all his co-religionists will be made to suffer.

Shalom further implies the establishment of sound and amicable relations with other communities, so that they can all work in full harmony.

I understand, from various sources, that the State of Indiana has not less than eighteen Jewish congregations, all zealous for the glory of God and active in the cause of Judaism. "The Lord God of your fathers make you a thousand times as many more as you are."

Now Shalom, like Charity, or Zedakah, begins at home, and I hope that it will be in your co-operation with the sister synagogues in the immediate neighborhood that the effects of this blessed work will be first seen. But this, naturally, is only the beginning. These relations of Shalom must extend further to the whole of the Keneseth Israel, the Congregation of Israel. Judaism has no geographical limits. It is as great as the world, and as wide as the universe, and you must avoid every action of a sectarian or of a schismatic nature, calculated to loosen the ties between you and your brethren scattered over our globe. In olden times the synagogues and the houses' of interpretation occasionally served as places offering accommodation to travelers. We have now different means of providing hospitality. But nothing must be done in the synagogue which would deter a Jew from seeking spiritual shelter. Our synagogues are, and must remain, as of old, "the tents of Jacob, and the dwelling place of Israel."

The last words of our text, *baer heteb*, demanding that the words on the stones of the altar be lucidly explained, gave rise, as you know, to the School of Sopherim, the scribes whose office it was to read the Book of the Law of God distinctly, giving the sense and causing the poeple to understand the reading. In time this activity resulted in the various Targumim, the versions in the Aramaic vernacular of Onkelos and Jonathan ben Uzziel, and into the Greek of Aquila, a pupil of R. Akiba. The mission of the modern Sopherim would accordingly be to explain the words of the Torah, the prophets, the Psalmists and the sages in the vernacular of today—which in this country is the English language. I can quite understand the attachment some of us feel toward the German-jargon, or *patois*—call it what you will— in which for so many centuries Jewish mothers wrote their Techinoth (supplications), and which is still spoken by such a large portion of Jewry. But let us beware lest we attach any sacredness to this dialect. America, some one rightly remarked, is the grave of languages. No foreign language, be it ever so rich in great masterpieces of literature survives a single generation in this country. The children of the immigrant who visit our public schools soon compel their parents to speak English. It would thus be a sin to attach the fortunes of our great literature to the fortunes of this language, which is a mere accident in our history, doomed to die, and is dying before our very eyes. We cannot, we dare not, endanger the Judaism of our children by making a virtue of what may have once been an unfortunate necessity, but at present, thank God, is becoming an impossibility.

On the other hand, it is not necessary to dwell here at length on the vital importance of Hebrew, the Sacred tongue. It is the great depository of all that is best in the soul-life of the Congregation of Israel. Without it we will become a mere sect, without a past, and without a literature, and without a proper Liturgy, and severed from the great Tree which is life unto those that cling to it. Hellenistic Judaism is the only one known to history which dared to make this experiment of dispensing with the Sacred Language. The result was death. It withered away and terminated in total and wholesale apostasy from Judaism. Let us not deceive ourselves. There is no future in this country for a Judaism that resists either the English or the Hebrew language.

In the course of the ages the scribe of old became the Rabbi of today. He reads and expounds the Law at the solemn convocations in the synagogues, applies it to the every-day needs and problems besetting the lives of the worshipers, and perpetuates it by teaching it diligently to the children of the community under his guidance. My friends, it is now my pleasant duty to introduce to you your Rabbi, my friend and disciple, Charles Isaiah Hoffman, whom the Faculty of the Jewish Theological Seminary of America has recently found worthy of such a high and holy office. He will cause the very stones of his edifice to preach to you loyalty to our Torah. He will become the Meturgeman, the Interpreter to this community of the ancient Jewish truth; his aim will ever be to bring the future generations under the wings of the Schechinah.

"May the beauty of the Lord our God be upon us; establish Thou the work of our hands upon us; yea, the work of our hands establish thou it. Amen."

ZIONISM: A STATEMENT.*

THERE is a story told of a German Jew of the
older generation that when his friends came to
him about the beginning of the "eighties" of the last
century, and asked what he thought of these *new*
attacks on the Jews, he looked rather astonished, and
said, "They are not new; they are the old ones." I
may say with equal justice that the attacks on Zionism which have come lately from press and pulpit
are not new. They have been refuted ever so many
times, and have been as often repeated. Lest, however, my ignoring direct challenges would, in accordance with the old rule, "Silence is tantamount to
admission," be taken as a proof that I have at last
become converted by the arguments of our opponents,
I will state here clearly the reasons for my allegiance
to Zionism. I wish only to premise that I am no
official expounder of Zionism. I am not claiming
or aspiring to the role of leadership in this movement.
The following remarks have only the value of representing the opinion of one of the rank and file, stating
clearly his attitude towards this movement, though
he believes that he reflects the views of a great number
of fellow Zionists.

Zionism is an ideal, and as such is indefinable.
It is thus subject to various interpretations and sus-
ceptive of different aspects. It may appear to one
as the rebirth of national Jewish consciousness, to

*First published in pamphlet form, December 28, 1906.

another as a religious revival, whilst to a third it may present itself as a path leading to the goal of Jewish culture; and to a fourth it may take the form of the last and only solution of the Jewish problem. By reason of this variety of aspects, Zionism has been able to unite on its platform the most heterogeneous elements; representing Jews of all countries, and exhibiting almost all the different types of culture and thought as only a really great and universal movement could command. That each of its representatives should emphasize the particular aspect most congenial to his way of thinking, and most suitable for his mode of action, is only natural. On one point, however, they all agree, namely, that it is not only desirable, but absolutely necessary, that Palestine, the land of our fathers, should be recovered with the purpose of forming a home for at least a portion of the Jews, who would lead there an independent national life. That the language of the leaders was sometimes ambiguous and not quite definite in the declaration of this principle is owing to the boldness of the proposition and the environments in which these leaders were brought up, where everything distinctly Jewish was in need of an apology, rather than to any doubt about the final aim of Zionism, as conceived in the minds of the great majority of Zionists. Nor was it strange that some backslidings should occur, and that in moments of despair, counsels of despair should prevail, considering the terrible crises through which we have passed during the last few years. The great majority of Zionists remain loyal to the great idea of Zion and

Jerusalem, to which history and tradition, and the general Jewish sentiment, point. It is "God's country" in the fullest and truest sense of the words. It is the "Promised Land" still maintaining its place in every Jewish heart, excepting those, perhaps, with whom Jewish history commences about the year 1830, and Jewish literature is confined to the transactions of the Rabbinical synods of the last century, and the files of Philippson's *Allgemeine Zeitung des Judenthums*.

To me personally, after long hesitation and careful watching, Zionism recommended itself as the great bulwark against assimilation. By assimilation I do not understand what is usually understand by Americanization: namely, that every Jew should do his best to acquire the English language; that he should study American history and make himself acquainted with the best productions of American literature; that he should be a law-abiding citizen, thoroughly appreciating the privilege of being a member of this great commonwealth, and joyfully prepared to discharge the duties of American citizenship. What I understand by assimilation is loss of identity; or that process of disintegration which, passing through various degrees of defiance of all Jewish thought and of disloyalty to Israel's history and its mission, terminates variously in different lands. In Germany, for instance (where the pressure from above in favor of the dominant religion is very strong), it ends in direct and public apostasy; in other countries where this pressure has been removed, it results in the severance of all affiliation with the synagogue, and is followed by a sort of "eclectic religiosity," that coquettes with the various churches, not neglecting even the Christian Science Temple, and is consummated by a final, though imperceptible, absorption in the great majority. This consummation will surely be hastened by the gradual disappearance of social disparity. What this process finally means for Judaism will perhaps be best seen from the following quotation from Wellhausen's *History of Israel*. After giving Spinoza's oft-quoted view regarding the possibilities of the absorption of Israel by its surroundings, the well-known Bible critic remarks: "The persistency of the race may, of course, prove a harder thing to overcome than Spinoza has supposed; but, nevertheless, he will be found to have spoken truly in declaring that the so-called emancipation of the Jews must inevitably lead to the extinction of Judaism wherever the process is extended beyond the political to the social sphere."

The only comfort that Wellhausen leaves us is that "for the accomplishment of this, centuries may be required." We, and the few generations that are to succeed us, are to cheerfully abide in this intermediate condition, and to acquiesce in the tortures of a slow death; or, as the great Alexandrian sage in his description of the punishment awaiting the specially wicked, expresses it, we are "to live continually dying," and to endure an unceasing dissolution until death will have mercy upon us and will give us the last *coup de grace.*

It is this kind of assimilation, with the terrible consequences indicated, that I dread most; even more than pogroms. To this form of assimilation, Zionism in the sense defined will prove, and is already proving a most wholesome check. Whatever faults may be found with its real or self-appointed leaders, Zionism as a whole forms an opposing force against the conception of the destiny of Israel and the interpretation of its mission, the leading thought of which is apparently the well-known epigram, "Whosoever shall seek to gain his life shall lose it, but whosoever shall lose his life shall preserve it." Zionism declares boldly to the world that Judaism means to preserve its life by *not* losing its life. It shall be a true and healthy life, with a policy of its own, a religion wholly its own, invigorated by sacred memories and sacred environments, and proving a tower of strength and of unity not only for the remnant gathered within the borders of the Holy Land, but also for those who shall, by choice or necessity, prefer what now constitutes the Galuth.

The term Galuth is here loosely used, expressing, as I have often heard it, the despair and helplessness felt in the presence of a great tragedy. And the tragedy is not imaginary. It is real, and it exists everywhere. It *is* a tragedy to see a great ancient people, distinguished for its loyalty to its religion, and its devotion to its sacred law, losing thousands every day by the mere process of attrition. It *is* a tragedy to see sacred institutions as ancient as the mountains, to maintain which Israel for thousands of years shrank from no sacrifice, destroyed before our very eyes and exchanged for corresponding institutions borrowed from hostile religions. It *is* a tragedy to see a language held sacred by all the world, in

which Holy Writ was composed, and which served as
the depository of Israel's greatest and best thought,
doomed to oblivion and forced out gradually from
the synagogue. It *is* a tragedy to see the descendants
of those who revealed revelation to the world and who
developed the greatest religious literature in existence,
so little familiar with real Jewish thought, and so
utterly wanting in all sympathy with it, that they have
no other interpretation to offer of Israel's scriptures,
Israel's religion, and Israel's ideals and aspirations
and hopes, than those suggested by their natural
opponents, slavishly following their opinions, copying
their phrases, repeating their catchwords, not sparing
us even the taunt of tribalism and Orientalism. I am
not accusing anybody. I am only stating facts that
are the outcome of causes under which we all labor,
but for none of which any party in particular can be
made responsible, though it cannot be denied that some
among us rather made too much virtue of a necessity,
and indulged, and are still indulging in experiments in
euthanasia. The economic conditions under which we
live; the innate desire for comfort; the inherent tendency towards imitation; the natural desire not to
appear peculiar; the accessibility of theological
systems, possessing all the seductions of "newness
and modernity," patronized by fashion and even by
potentates, and taught in ever so many universities,
and condensed in dozens of encyclopedias, are
sufficient and weighty enough causes to account for
our tragedy. But, however natural the causes may
be, they do not alter the doom. The effects are bound
to be fatal. The fact thus remains that we are help-

less spectators in the face of great tragedies, in other words, that we are in Galuth. This may not be the Galuth of the Jews, but it is the Galuth of Judaism, or, as certain mystics expressed it, the Galuth of *Hannephesh*, the Galuth of the Jewish soul wasting away before our very eyes. With a little modification we might repeat here the words of a Jewish Hellenist of the second century who, in his grief, exclaims: "Wherefore is Israel given up as a reproach to the heathen, and for what cause is the people whom Thou best loved given unto ungodly nations, and why is the law of our forefathers brought to naught, and the written covenants come to none effect? And we pass away out of the world as grasshoppers, and our life is astonishment and fear, and we are not worthy to obtain mercy."

The foregoing remarks have made it clear that I belong to that class of Zionists that lay more stress on the religious-national aspects of Zionism than on any other feature peculiar to it. The rebirth of Israel's national consciousness, and the revival of Israel's religion, or, to use a shorter term, the revival of Judaism, are inseparable. When Israel found itself, it found its God. When Israel lost itself, or began to work at its self-effacement, it was sure to deny its God. The selection of Israel, the indestructibility of God's covenant with Israel, the immortality of Israel as a nation, and the final restoration of Israel to Palestine, where the nation will live a holy life on holy ground, with all the wide-reaching consequences of the conversion of humanity and the establishment of the Kingdom of God on earth—all these are the

common ideals and the common ideas that permeate
the whole of Jewish literature extending over nearly
four thousand years, including the largest bulk of the
Hellenistic portion of it.　The universalistic passages
in the Scripture usually paraded by the "prophetic
Jew" as implying the final disappearance, or extinction of Israel, are in every case misquotations torn
from their context, or ignoring other utterances by
the same writer.　Indeed, our prophetic Jew

> "Boldly pilfers from the Pentateuch:
> And, undisturbed by conscientious qualms,
> Perverts the Prophets, and purloins the Psalms."

The interpretations smuggled into the passages are
just as false and unscientific as the well-known Chris-
tological passages extracted from the Old Testament,
and even from the Talmud, to be met with in missionary tracts, composed especially for the benefit
of fresh converts.

The reproach that Zionism is unspiritual is meaningless.　Indeed, there seems to be a notion abroad
that spirituality is a negative quality.　Take any
ideal, and translate it into action, any sentiment of
reverence, and piety, and give it expression through
a symbol or ceremony, speak of the human yearning
after communion with God, and try to realize it
through actual prayer, and you will be at once de-
nounced as unspiritual.　However, the imputation is
as old as the days when the name Pharisee became a
reproach, and it is not to be expected that the Zionists
would be spared.　In general, it is the antinominian
who will tell you that he is the only heir to the rare
quality of spirituality, whereas the real saint is in

all his actions so spontaneous and so natural that he is entirely unconscious of possessing spirituality, and practically never mentions it.

The Zionists are no saints, but they may fairly claim that few movements are more free from the considerations of convenience and comfort, and less tainted with worldliness and other worldliness than the one which they serve. Nothing was to be gained by joining it. All the powers that be, were, and still are, opposed to it, whether in their capacity as individuals or as wealthy corporations. The Zionists are just beginning to be tolerated, but I remember distinctly the time when adhesion to the cause of Zionism might interfere with the prospects of a man's career, the cry being, "no Zionists need apply." The classes from which the Zionists were recruited were mostly the poorest among the poor. College men and university men, more blessed with enthusiasm and idealism than with the goods of this world, also furnished a fair quota. But this lack of means did not prevent them from responding most generously to every appeal made on behalf of the cause. They taxed themselves to the utmost of their capacity, and beyond. I myself have witnessed cases in which men and women joyfully contributed their last earnings, foregoing their summer vacations, for which they had been saving a whole year.

The activity of Zionism must not be judged by what it has accomplished *in* Zion and Jerusalem— where it has to deal with political problems as yet not ripe for solution—but by what it has thus far achieved *for* Zion and Jerusalem, through the awaken-

ing of the national Jewish consciousness, notwithstanding the systematic and ruthless efforts made in
the opposite direction during the greater part of the
last century. Our synagogues and our homes plainly
show the effect. Zion and Jerusalem have not been
allowed to stand as a sad, glorious remembrance of
a past, as mere objects of pious sentiment. Indeed,
the astounding discovery was made that far from
being considered as a day of disaster, the Ninth
of Ab has to be looked upon as a day of liberation,
when Judaism threw off the shackles of nationalism
to congeal into a mere Church—with a ritual and a
body of doctrines to be promulgated some nineteen
hundred years later. Unfortunately, Israel was
smitten with blindness, failing to understand its real
destiny, and in the perversion of its heart, for eighteen
hundred years observed the Ninth of Ab as a day of
mourning and weeping, of humiliation and fasting,
thus wilfully delaying its redemption. I have always
wondered that the Church was not yet enterprising
enough to put up a statue in gratitude to its benefactor
Titus, the *delectus generis humani*, representing the
goddess *Universa*, with a scribe and a priest cowering
in chains at her feet.

The work, accordingly, in which Zionism had to
engage first, and in which it will have to continue for
many years to come, was the work of regeneration.
It had to re-create the Jewish consciousness before
creating the Jewish state. In this respect, Zionism
has already achieved great things. There is hardly a
single Jewish community in any part of the globe
which is not represented by a larger or smaller num-

ber of men and women acknowledging themselves as
Zionists and standing out as a living protest against
the tendencies just hinted at. It has created a press,
and has called into life a host of lecturers and speakers
propagating its doctrines and preaching them boldly
to Israel all over the world. It has given the world
Asher Ginzberg, or, as he is better known, by the
pen name of Achad Ha-am, one of our finest intellects
and most original thinkers; and he is followed by a
whole host of disciples, all of them working under the
stimulus of the Jewish national ideal, much as they
may differ in the Zionistic aspects they happen to
emphasize. It has enriched our literature with a
large number of novels and lyrics, and even distinct
Zionist melodies are not wanting. It has further
called into existence numerous societies, whose aim
it is to make the sacred tongue a living language
by means of writing and even conversing in it, while
in several communities special schools have been
established with the same end in view. To better
advance this end, a whole series of Hebrew primers,
grammars and reading books for the young have been
produced. Several translations prepared from German, French and English works bearing on Jewish
history and cognate subjects, all of them calculated
to strengthen religious-national consciousness, have
also appeared under the inspiration of Zionism. Foremost of all, Zionism has succeeded in bringing back
into the fold many men and women, both here and
in Europe, who otherwise would have been lost to
Judaism. It has given them a new interest in the
synagogue and everything Jewish, and put before

them an ideal worthy of their love and their sacrifice.
Cases have come under my notice where Jewish college men, at a comparatively advanced age, began
to study the sacred language and to repair to the
synagogue, sharing both in its joys and in its griefs,
some among them encountering the displeasure and
ridicule of their relatives, who were fanatical assim-
ilators and who bring up their children without
religious education of any kind. Of course, backslidings and relapses occur; but it is an advantage
to Zionism that in its present condition, at least,
it is all sacrifice and no gain. It holds out no prospect
to the ambitious and to "those who exalt themselves
to establish the vision" of a Jewish state without
Jewish memories, without historic foundation and
without traditional principles. The undesirables
and the impatient will thus, under one pretense or
another, leave it soon, and indeed are dropping out
already, so that its purification of all alloy and discordant elements is only a question of a very short time.

The taunt of retrogression and reaction has no
terrors for us. To insist on progressing when one has
come to the conclusion that a step forward means ruin
is sheer obstinacy. Unless we are convinced so deeply
of our infallibility that we take every utterance of
ours as a divine revelation, and our every action as
a precedent and a tradition, there may come a time
in our lives when we may have to return. As a
fact, Zionism is the natural rebound from an artificial
and overstrained condition of things which could
no longer last. It is the Declaration of Jewish
Independence from all kinds of slavery, whether

material or spiritual. It is as natural and instinctive as life itself, and no amount of scolding and abuse will prevent the reassertion of the Jewish soul which in our unconscious Zionism is an actual present-day experience, though the expression given to it takes different shape in different minds. Moreover, Zionism thoroughly believes in progress and development; but it must be progress along Jewish lines, and the goal to be reached must be the Jewish historic ideal.

But, whilst Zionism is constantly winning souls for the present, it is at the same time preparing for us the future, which will be a Jewish future. Only then, when Judaism has found itself, when the Jewish soul has been redeemed from the Galuth, can Judaism hope to resume its mission to the world. Everybody whose view has not been narrowed by the blinkers imposed on him by his little wing or by party considerations, knows well enough that it is not only traditional religion which is on trial. We are on a veritable volcano created by the upheavals of the newest methods of "searching research," which respects as little the new formulae, such as the categoric imperative, conscience, the notion of duty and the concept of morality and ethics, as it does creeds and dogmas. The disruption may come at any moment unless revelation is reasserted. The declaration, *Freedom is our Messiah*, which I have so often heard, may be good Fourth of July oratory, but it is miserably bad theology, and worse philosophy, having in view the terrible woes and complicated problems besetting humanity. Now, what happened once may happen again, and Israel may another time be called

upon with its mission to the nations. Under the
present conditions, however, we have neither a defined mission, nor does any man take this "mission"
seriously, and the talk about it is allowed to be a
mere *licencia predicatorum*. But we know that the
Bible which influenced humanity so deeply and
proved so largely instrumental in the partial conversion of the world, arose in Palestine or in circles
which looked on Palestine as their home. Those who
wrote the Bible moved and had their whole being
in the religious national idea, and lived under the
discipline of the Law. History may, and to my
belief, will repeat itself, and Israel will be the chosen
instrument of God for the new and final mission; but
then Israel must first effect its own redemption and
live again its own life, and be Israel again, to accomplish its universal mission. The passages in the Bible
most distinguished for their universalistic tendency
and grandeur are, as is well known, the verses in
Isaiah and Micah, and there it is solemnly proclaimed: "Out of Zion shall go forth the law, and
the word of the Lord from Jerusalem."

Our sages have themselves given expression to
this correspondence between the universalistic and
the nationalistic elements in Judaism. A solemn
declaration, thus they declare, has the Holy One,
blessed be He, registered: "I will not enter the heavenly Jerusalem, until Israel shall come to the earthly
Jerusalem." Not in conflict but in consonance with
Israel's establishment of the divine institutions in
their full integrity in God's own land, will be the
triumph in all its glory of the Kingdom of Heaven.

THE PROBLEM OF RELIGIOUS EDUCATION.*

M Y Friends: It is now the fourth time that we meet in this hall to participate in the commencement exercises of this Seminary. Our pleasant task will be to do honor to those to whom honor is due, conferring the degree of Rabbi on some, the degree of Doctor on others, and awarding prizes to those who, by their particular industry and devotion to learning deserve this distinction. It is, to my knowledge, the first time that the Seminary confers the Doctor Degree for work done, upon which occasion I congratulate both the faculty and the directors. The importance of this degree consists in the fact that it shows that our students do not rest satisfied with that title which enables them to perform the necessary functions in their respective Synagogues, but that they endeavor to continue their studies, the foundations of which were laid at the Seminary.

In a previous graduation address, I had occasion to speak of the various activities of the Rabbi and the different needs of the community which a Rabbi is expected to superintend. I propose to offer a few remarks on this solemn occasion on the subject of Talmud Torah. By Talmud Torah I do not mean the study of Jewish literature as pursued by the Rabbi and the few professional students. The Talmud

---

*Address delivered at the Graduating Exercises of the Seminary, June 2, 1907.

Torah of which I wish to speak on this occasion is the study of the Torah, extended to the humblest member of the community, reaching the very babes; or, as the term is commonly used as a synonym of the בית הספר (the public school). In this capacity the Talmud Torah is one of the main objects for which synagogues are built and Rabbis are appointed. Thus, Judges 5:11 is paraphrased by an ancient Rabbi, "Here is a small settlement in Israel. And they rose and built a synagogue and appointed a sage and engaged teachers for the children. The good example is followed by another city in its neighborhood. They also built a synagogue and engaged teachers. And so the schools increase in Israel, in which the righteous acts of the Lord are rehearsed even in the very villages." The establishment of a school for children, or the erection of the Talmud Torah, and equipping it with the necessary staff is here regarded as the main function of the synagogue. This was the rule which was followed by Israel almost throughout its long history. No community was too small to provide for the instruction of the young, and no sacrifice was too great.

How deeply this sentiment took root in Israel may be seen by the various references to bequests for the Talmud Torah scattered over the *Responsa* of the Middle Ages and other historical records. In a *Responsum* dating from the sixteenth century, mention is made of a single bequest of one hundred thousand *lebenim* for educational purposes. This would be a princely donation even in our own times, considering the purchasing value of money in the sixteenth century, which was about fifteen times as much as it is at present. The first task, again, which the Jewish community at Amsterdam, entirely consisting of refugees from various parts of Europe, set to itself was the building up of a model school. Rabbi Sheftel Horwitz, of Frankfort, a place more distinguished at that period for its piety and erudition than for system and method, shed tears of joy when he visited the school, with its fine building, its graded schedule, and its excellent discipline, and recommended it as a model to his fellow-countrymen, the German Jews. The community of Cracow, again, in the sixteenth century, after passing through terrible epidemics, took the first opportunity after its return to normal conditions to reorganize its schools, which, coinciding with the distress of the times, was only done at a great sacrifice on the part of its members.

However, it is not my intention to dwell here upon the history of the Talmud Torah and its various improvements, which may easily be found in a number of books dealing with this subject. All I want to urge is, first, that the Talmud Torah is an essential adjunct to the Synagogue. Secondly, that it is just after great historical catastrophes that the importance of the Talmud Torah is even more realized than before, and forms a main feature in the programme of the newly settled or reorganized congregations. The school children are, as the Rabbis suggest, the very "flower and blossom of the Courts of our Lord," so that the synagogue and the establishment of the Talmud Torah in a sorely tried community means a new pledge for the rejuvenation of Israel. The conditions of a great part of Jewry in America are in many respects not dissimilar to those of the Amsterdam community. Our numbers consist chiefly of immigrants fleeing from conditions resembling those of Europe in the seventeenth century, and like those refugees, we are also engaged in the process of the creation of our institutions. Much has been done of which every American Jew can be truly proud. Our places of worship and our charitable institutions, which are constantly increasing in number and in weight, bear comparison with those of the oldest communities in Europe and Asia. But there is one sore point which requires the serious attention of our leaders, and that is the Talmud Torah. I by no means overlook the fact that we are already in possession of institutions set apart for the purpose of training Rabbis and devoted to the cause of higher Jewish learning. To those already in existence, a new one is to be added by the munificence of the late Moses A. Dropsie, at Philadelphia, under the direction of experienced guides and trusted leaders, whose work, I have no doubt, will likewise contribute to magnify the cause of Jewish learning and to make it glorious.

Yet it must be stated that as long as we have no proper Talmud Torah, the higher learning will always remain without a basis and never take root on American soil. The normal conditions in olden times seem to have been that of a thousand persons entering the Talmud Torah, the largest number obtained a fair knowledge of the Bible, a smaller number became acquainted with the Mishnah and a certain fraction even acquired a knowledge of the Talmud; whilst it was only one of a thousand who was considered capable of giving decisions, or as we would say, of exercising the functions of the Rabbi in the widest sense of the word. We have fairly provided for the one in a thousand, but have done very little for the remaining nine hundred and ninety-nine. I by no means ignore the existence of our Sunday Schools, in addition to a certain number of Talmud Torah schools and a large number of private tutors in religion, or Melamdim, but they are quite out of proportion to the numbers which are left without any religious instruction. In a conversation lately with a gentleman familiar with the statistics of New York, I learned to my surprise that there must be at least 150,000 Jewish children in New York, and that the provision for religious instruction, by rough calculation, hardly amounts to the relief even of the third part of this number. These are alarming conditions. But what is worse is that we could hardly supply the deficiency even if we had the will, for we are still to a large extent lacking in everything indispensable for the building up of the Talmud Torah.

The first difficulty under which we labor is the great dearth of trained teachers. The old private tutor, or Melamed, is an impossibility in this country for any length of time. Judging by results which held good for many centuries, it would be hazardous to say that his method was entirely wrong. However, great as the results may have been to which he can point in former generations and under different conditions, it is not likely that he will be able to maintain his status much longer. Neither his medium of instruction nor his method is to be recommended in the case of boys brought up in an American public school. It is especially his medium of instruction which is a thing impossible in this country, and sooner or later it must give way to the English language, the language of our fellow-citizens, the language of the public schools, and the language of all other institutions of learning. The American teacher, with his knowledge of the English language and his familiarity with the best educational methods, will thus in the end prove to be the only fit person to instruct also in religion, but unfortunately he is not always sufficiently equipped with a knowledge of Hebrew things in general and the Hebrew language in particular, to enable him to accomplish his duties in a satisfactory manner. A thorough and sound knowledge of Hebrew is an indispensable qualification of every teacher in a Jewish religious school. It is the sacred language, it is the language of the Bible, it is the language of the Prayer Book and the despository of all the sublimest thoughts and noblest sentiments that Israel taught and felt for more than three thousand years. It is the tie that unites us with millions of worshippers in the same sacred language, who are our brothers and our brethren in spite of all the latest theological discoveries and ethnological hypotheses. It is the natural language of the Jew when in communion with his God; he divines more than he is able to explain. Translations are a poor makeshift at best, and more often a miserable caricature. For more than twenty-three centuries the world has been busy with the interpretation and translation of the Scriptures, and yet no agreement has been reached as to the exact rendering of the fourth verse of the sixth chapter of Deuteronomy containing the confession of Israel's creed. But the Jew reads the שמע ישראל and does know it. He cannot translate it, but he feels it and *is* it. For, as the mystics have it, to be a thing is to know a thing, and to know a thing is to be a thing.

I am aware that there are some well-meaning persons who maintain that the fate of religion should not be made dependent on a certain language. The real question is what we mean by religion. If we are indifferent as to the nature of the religion (confusing it with religiosity) any language will do. It may blossom out into an ethical cult, it may develop into the worship of the beautiful and the sublime, or may take the shape of the Service of Man. Constituted, however, as human nature is, with its hankering after the mysterious and its tendency towards the worship of Sorrow, it is more probable that this "distilled religion" will sooner or later evaporate into a sort of Spiritualism or Christian Science. Of this possibility the signs are not wanting even at the present moment. But whatever shape it may take, it will certainly not be Judaism. When the last sound of Hebrew will have disappeared from our synagogues, the last trace of Judaism will also have gone.

We must thus insist upon Hebrew. But for this we require proper training schools. All our means at present are of a perfunctory nature and accomplish

very little. The Seminary has with inadequate means
tried to cope with this difficulty, but I do not think
that it will ever accomplish this mission without
increasing its staff of teachers for this purpose, and
extending its curriculum and the number of hours of
instruction. But above all, no training can be perfect
without the help of a model school in which the teachers should impart instruction for a certain number
of years under the supervision of their professors.

The second crying need is the almost utter lack
of text-books. Through some cause or other, the
English language is the poorest in this kind of literature. We have as yet no Jewish history fit to place
in the hands of a teacher or pupil, no readers for the
different grades, and no commentary to the Bible
written in a Jewish spirit. I am glad to announce
on this occasion that the Jewish Publication Society,
recognizing this last want, is now engaged in the preparation of such a commentary as will undoubtedly
have the effect of bringing the Bible back to the Jew.
We must have a whole series of primers and readers
and text-books and histories extending at least over
a course of eight years, commencing with the Hebrew
alphabet and culminating somewhere in the later
Hebrew literature. I cannot refrain on this occasion
from paying my tribute to our brethren in Russia,
who amidst all the persecutions by which these last
decades have been marked, have produced a large
educational literature covering almost all the subjects
fit for instruction, which excites the envy and admiration of every student. It is humiliating to think
that with all the means at our disposal and our various

societies constantly discussing the topic I am just dealing with, we should be in this respect behind our brethren in the East, the poorest among the poor, and engaged in a deadly struggle with all the powers of darkness.

But it is only when we have provided for the needs of the nine hundred and ninety-nine, by well-equipped training schools for teachers and proper text-books in the English language, fit to be put in the hands of the so-called laity, that the mission of the thousandth (that of the Rabbi) will be accomplished. Without this broad basis of the congregation at large, and its hearty co-operation, the work of the Rabbi will never be effective. The knowledge of the one will never be able to grapple successfully with the ignorance of the many. The old saying was, "Knowledge is Power." Paradox as it may seem, everyone will admit that Ignorance is a greater Power—on the side of destruction. I do not hesitate for a moment to maintain that the excesses in the camp of Judaism which we witness, and this unceasing succession of spiritual amputations which is going on before our very eyes, is mainly owing to the insufficient acquaintance with the tenets of Judaism, its traditions of the past and its aspirations and hopes for the future on the part of the nine hundred and ninety-nine. Never before were the words of the Prophet so fully realized, "My people are destroyed for lack of knowledge: because thou hast rejected knowledge, I will also reject thee, that thou shalt be no priest to me: seeing that thou hast forgotten the Law of thy God, I will also forget thy children." (Hos. 4:6)

We are laboring under the peculiar idea that we shall benefit Judaism by removing the last vestige of the Sabbath, by abolishing the Day of Atonement, or robbing it of its most essential features, by banishing the Sefer Torah from the place of worship, and by removing the last shreds of the sacred language. This seems to be the programme of the twentieth century, and this is what we call progress in Judaism. Nay, we hail it as hastening the day in which "the upright shall exult, and the saints triumphantly rejoice,"—the day which formed one of Israel's brightest visions and the object of Israel's prayers for thousands of years. It never occurs to us that this irreverence for the past, this perpetual battering away at institutions considered sacred by the great majority of mankind, this worship of individualism which in most cases is nothing more than thinly disguised selfishness and vanity, and this disregard of authority and the utter absence of the qualities of submission and obedience are, in part at least, responsible for the rampant materialism and unrighteousness which we all so much deplore.

A great European thinker somewhere remarked, "America, with its lack of high culture, is the only nation in our day which has been able to furnish soil for new religions." This is a malicious libel. A country which has given to the world men of the stamp of Emerson, Channing, Lowell, Motley, and so many other celebrities, can in all respects compare favorably with any part of the Old World; but I cannot help saying that my heart fails me when I see the mushroom religions springing up around us,

the constant travesties and caricatures of the Bible
which we are witnessing, and the assurance with which
men offer their undigested thoughts as substitutes
for religion. As to the experiments to which Judaism
is often subjected, the least one can say is that they
show that our knowledge of religion and the great
historical forces at work in the spiritual world are
of an amateur order. Be an idea ever so absurd, be
it ever so incompatible with all laws of history and
philosophy, ever so antagonistic to the spirit of Judaism and its teachings, it will always find a response
among us, provided it has eloquence and smartness
on its side, and is uttered with that certainty and
assurance which ignorance alone can command.

My young friends, ere long you will be active in
Jewish communities. Your activities will be arduous
and manifold. Holiness as understood by Judaism,
and righteousness as understood by Judaism and by
the large bulk of humanity will be the subjects that
will occupy your attention. But never forget the
Talmud Torah. Do apply yourselves to the training
of the nine hundred and ninety-nine, so that they may
be in time your equals in the knowledge of Judaism.
Be not afraid that a universal knowledge of the
Scriptures and of the important works embodying
Jewish tradition and Jewish history will in any way
curtail your authority. The Sabbath preceding the
Day of Atonement and the one preceding the Passover
were, as you know, the fete days of the Synagogue,
when the Rabbi would give lengthy discourses on
some complicated Halachic subjects. Both the pupils
and the members of the Congregation were permitted

to take part in the discussion, but none felt prouder than the Rabbi if one of his congregants would stop him with the words, "Master, you have overlooked a paragraph in Maimonides' Code," or, "Master, according to your argument this or that passage in the Novelae of Rabbi Solomon ben Adereth would be quite unintelligible," for such contradiction on the part of the so-called "laity" showed that the work of the Rabbi was effective, and that he and his predecessors had done their duty by the community with regard to Talmud Torah. This is the pride which you ought to cultivate, and make it the goal of your ambition. It is a poor sort of authority which derives its infallibility from the helplessness of the majority. The authority that maintains itself by the ignorance of the masses is not worth having.

One of the most important characteristics of the synagogue was its democratic constitution, placing everybody under the law and making the knowledge of the law accessible to all. Under the law, we are all equals; outside of the law, or, as it is called, above the law, is anarchy and confusion, resulting in tyranny. In politics, we are overwhelmed by the dragoon; in the spiritual world, we are crushed by the talker. My friends, restore to the synagogue its democratic spirit. Remain in the service of the law, and do not aspire to be above the law. This is not spirituality; this is conspiracy. In the synagogue everybody taught, everybody learned, everybody contributed his or her share in its building up, in its aspect as a collection of institutions making for the sanctification of life in its various manifestations. To hand over one's conscience and things most sacred to a single individual, be he ever so great, brands one as a "slave by his own compulsion," or as indifferent to the cause of religion. This is neither American nor Jewish. Remember, my friends, the words of Maimonides: "The guarantee for the survival of Judaism is the continuance of the knowledge of God's Torah and the acquaintance with His word among us." With the disappearance of the Torah, the synagogue itself can become a danger to itself and a playground for all the forces of destruction. It may cease to be a Beth Hakneseth, suggestive of the Keneseth Israel, where the spirit of Catholic Israel dwells, and become a בית עם (the House of the Plebs), where multitudes enjoy "intellectual treats," even at the very expense of Judaism. Only knowledge of Judaism can ward off this danger. For thus it is written:

> "They shall not hurt nor destroy in all my holy mountain: for the earth shall be full of the knowledge of the Lord, as the waters cover the sea."

MORITZ STEINSCHNEIDER.*

THE year 1907 brought many a bereavement to the Jewish student. It is sufficient to mention here the names of Solomon Buber, the great editor and interpreter of the Midrashic literature; Dr. Adolph Neubauer, the compiler of the catalogue of the Hebrew manuscripts in the Oxford libraries, and Professor Jacob Freudenthal, one of the very few Jewish students who made the study of (Hellenistic) literature the subject of their thorough researches. But the death of none came so unexpectedly as that of Moritz Steinschneider. That the immortal Steinschneider should ever die, that the man whom every Jewish student for more than two generations was in the habit of consulting first, when approaching a new subject, should ever be removed from the stage of his great activity, was something for which we were hardly prepared. He lived with all of us, and he survived so many of us, that one could rather think of having one's own death some day recorded by Steinschneider in one of his bibliographical notices, than to write his obituary.

Nor is this task a very easy one, considering that his life extended over ninety-one years, and that it was all activity. As of the great "scribe of the law," it may also be said of him that his vision never became dimmed, and that his freshness never dis-

*Paper presented at the Annual Meeting of the American Jewish Historical Society, 1908.

appeared until his dying day. Moreover, this activity
was not confined to a single branch of Jewish literature. His main attention seems to have been directed to the works of the Jewish philosophers, certain
of which he edited and all of which he fully described.
But this did not prevent him from being interested
in such subjects as the Jewish share in the secular
sciences, or the Jewish controversies with Moham-
medans and Christians, or the Jewish contributions
to the pseudographic literature of the world and
similar topics.

In consideration of these facts, I must refer you
for a real appreciation of Steinschneider's genius, and
the importance of his literary activity, to the admirable introduction to Steinschneider's *Gesammelte
Werke* by Drs. Malter and Marx. Here only a few
general remarks must suffice. As I have just said,
Steinschneider lived ninety-one years. His early
youth thus brings us back to the so-called *Measphim*
period, the period of the Jewish rationalists. These
were mostly recruited from Mendelssohn's disciples,
or those who believed themselves to be his disciples,
whose productions are embodied in the periodical
called *Ha-Measeph.* These publications are distinguished by the fine Hebrew style in which they were
written, which style, however, seems to have been
meant to cover a multitude of cheap rationalistic
platitudes, appearing to us almost childish and value-
less. Mendelssohn was of course their patron saint,
but they also claimed, as indeed many a superficial
theologian does to this day, Maimonides and a few
other Spanish Rabbis as their own. History was for

them non-existent. The few who dabbled in history, such as Peter Beer and his friends, showed only their utter impotence. Bishop Stubbs, the famous historian of the English Constitution, made a remark somewhere that no "dissenter" could ever write a good history of the English people and their institutions, as for them England only commences with Cromwell and other heroes of the Reformation. This may also be applied to the Jewish "dissenters" and their successors up to date, with whom Jewish history only begins with Mendelssohn. The reaction, or rather progress, came soon, represented by such men as Rapoport, Krochmal, and Zunz, who, with all their admiration for Mendelssohn, knew that Jewish history began somewhere in pre-historic times, that it was never interrupted by any circumstance, and that even the Middle Ages, with their long suffering and the darkness, covering the greater part of our globe, contributed their legitimate share of Jewish thought and Jewish activity to this history. Against all fashion of the time, Krochmal showed how the Talmud, the very *bête noir* of these rationalists, could be made an available source for this history. Rapoport did the same thing for the *Responsa* of the Geonim and other mediaeval productions, whilst Zunz, among other things, set himself to show the world what the Rabbis of the Franco-German schools contributed to Jewish thought, both in their commentaries on the Bible and the Talmud. He even showed that there is a great deal to learn from the Piyutim, the liturgical contributions of the mediaeval Rabbis, who were then the special subject of abuse by those who believed that the depth of devotion stands in inverse ratio to the length of the prayers. All these men were attacked in their turn by the rationalists, but truth and broadness of view conquered in the end. Even Abraham Geiger largely followed their lead, though he was never able to entirely forget that he was the leader of the opposition busy in composing "protocols" upsetting history.

Steinschneider was, to use a Talmudical term, "the fellow-disciple of all these great men." He learnt from Krochmal, though I am not certain that he ever saw him, but he attended the lectures of Rapoport in Prague, and was a close and intimate friend of Zunz, whom he followed in almost every detail in his famous sketch of Jewish literature, which we possess now in three versions, German, English and Hebrew. But, like all "fellow-disciples," he was not a mere reproducer of the works of his masters, but supplemented them greatly, and it was this supplementary work which became so important for the great majority of students.

It is true that some of Steinschneider's most important works aimed chiefly, as Drs. Malter and Marx rightly point out, at showing the position of the Jew in the literature of the world at large. We need here only point to Steinschneider's "Contributions of the Jews to Mathematics," "Contributions of the Jew to Medicine," and his work, "The Jews as translators and interpreters," etc., but these works are chiefly meant for the specialist of the sciences in question. The work by which he will after all be best remembered, and which has become the Urim and Thummim of every Jewish student, is his catalogue of the Bodleian Library and his other numerous contributions to Jewish bibliography. The bibliographer is, as is well known, the forerunner of the historian, for it is only when you know the sources of your subject and their sequence, that you can form a notion of the genesis and development of thought, and this was the great gift which Steinschneider bestowed on every one of us in dozens of volumes. Let any student who is anxious to write about the thought of a given period, try to dispense with Steinschneider, and he will find out at once how many anachronisms he will commit in the short space of a single generation.

As a bibliographer, Steinschneider was strictly "objective" or impartial. You cannot, with all the sympathy in the world, alter or interpret a single date in favor of a given theory or of a popular person. This impartiality is also manifest in all his other works, where he deals more with systems and theories than with dates and periods. Indeed, he was so impartial, that he occasionally became unjust, as, for instance, when he only lately attacked his friend and disciple, Professor David Kaufmann, on account of his using the term Jewish heroes and similar hyperbolic metaphors. It may also be that Steinschneider never entirely emancipated himself from the rationalism of his youth, or rather boyhood, when there was so little sympathy for Jewish heroism and so little understanding of that quality of Holiness, a distinguished feature of Jewish great men and Jewish great women, that was entirely misconceived and misrepresented by the generation which followed Voltaire. However, it is not for us of a later generation, who never knew the struggle, to criticise the

man from whom we learned so much. His peculiarities and his occasional attacks on men whom we admire
and revere, will soon enough be forgotten. They were
only accidental with him and formed by no means
a part of his system. He fortunately never accepted
any system in its entirety, and never joined in any
movement. Nay, everybody familiar with his works
knows that he was thoroughly suspicious of all those
systems and movements in Bible criticism and interpretations of Jewish history which are now the subject of heated controversy. He was skeptic enough
to question skepticism itself, but he left us quite
enough of what is positive, constructive and instructive in all departments of Jewish thought and Jewish
literature to render his name a blessing for all time.
But it must be a special source of satisfaction to this
Society, of which Steinschneider was an honorary
member, to know that his name will be particularly
connected with our great country. For, thanks to
the munificence of the Honorable Jacob H. Schiff,
Steinschneider's library now forms a part of the
collection of the Jewish Theological Seminary of
America. His books are full of annotations, containing untold treasures for the Jewish student. It also
deserves special mention that it is two American
scholars, Dr. Malter, of the Hebrew Union College.
of Cincinnati (now of the Dropsie College, Philadelphia), and Dr. Marx, of the Jewish Theological
Seminary of America, whom Steinschneider entrusted
with the edition of his *Gesammelle Schriften* to appear
in five volumes. His memory will thus never disappear from among the Jews, but will be especially
connected with American Judaism.

RABBI AS A PERSONAL EXAMPLE.*

IT IS now the fifth time that we meet in this hall to participate in the commencement exercises of the Seminary. The pleasant duty with which we have just been occupied was to confer degrees upon seven of our graduates. The labor was long, extending over years, and the work was by no means easy, covering a multitude of subjects demanding serious study and close application, but the reward has come at last in the shape of degrees just conferred—the only reward in the gift of the authorities of this institution.

But my young friends, do not flatter yourselves that your labors are at an end. They are only beginning. There is a story of an ancient Rabbi who warned his pupils when they were about to enter upon the performance of their duties, as follows: "Believe not that I make you masters: behold, you are appointed servants." The words sound harsh, but they contain a great truth which is often overlooked in our times, and that is—that no man in authority is greater than the source whence his authority is derived. The authority of the Rabbi is derived from the Torah; he is its servant, not its master. He may claim obedience to his teachings by the authority of the Torah, or כה התורה as the Hebrew phrase is, but he has no power over the

---

*Address delivered at the Graduating Exercises of the Seminary, June 7, 1908.

Torah. The mystical prayer *Berich Sh'meh*, read in most congregations by the Rabbi before the open ark, contains the following solemn declaration:

אנא עבדא דקודשא בריך הוא דסגידנא קמה ומקמה
דיקר אוריתה בכל עדן ועדן

"I am the servant of the Holy One, blessed be He, before whom and before whose glorious Law I prostrate myself at all times." The Torah is the inheritance of the Congregation of Jacob, not the possession of a single individual, and the Rabbi is not only responsible to his congregation, but to the whole of Israel for its preservation and perpetuation. This is indeed a most important principle in the democratic constitution of Israel, which both in the State and in the Synagogue considers the man holding a responsible office the servant of the institution and not its master. He belongs to the institution, not the institution to him. And to be the servant of the Torah means to labor in the Torah, to be constant learners as long as you remain constant teachers.

And be not niggardly in these labors, even after you have found favor with your congregation. And be not particularly exalted by the general applause. In fact, you ought to become a little distrustful of yourself under such circumstances. You well know that our ancient sages looked with some suspicion on the over-popularity of the Rabbi with his community, thinking as they did that it might be the result of his failing to admonish his flock in matters of heaven.

Indeed, admonition is necessary, for we are now in the midst of a great religious crisis, which is

occupying all thoughtful minds in this country, and
for which we all are seeking a remedy. The Rabbi,
as the spiritual leader of the community, will undoubtedly have to take his share in this struggle
against the evils of the day, which need not be detailed
here, and from which we are all suffering. Both in
the pulpit and on the platform, you will have to raise
your voice against the evils threatening the moral
progress of a country, which, by reason of its free
institutions, its exalted position and great power and
influence, should have become the light of nations.
But you cannot rely much on your voice. A sweet
voice, a pleasant manner and agreeable gestures are
no doubt helpful to the Rabbi. So is a rich vocabulary and an interesting topic. The graces of oratory
and the utmost power in your pulpit work will,
however, only then attain to real efficiency and practical results when the Rabbi not only says the right
thing, but also when he *is* the right thing. The right
thing the Rabbi should be is well defined by the
"Book of Saints," where we read, "The Rabbis must
be God-fearing men." Lest you th'nk the passage
just quoted a malicious innuendo on the sacred calling
you are about to enter upon, I will remind you of
another passage closely connected with it, "It is the
man who possesses the virtue of the fear of God,
whose words find a ready hearing." Tested by this
result, you will agree that this virtue is not so general
as commonly imagined. People will listen to you
willingly enough when your teaching is of a negative
nature. The applause of the world will seldom fail
you when you set out on the career of destruction

and proceed to abolish the one or the other law, and
startle the public by some sensational paradoxes
hostile to the teachings of Judaism. And the praise
of the thoughtless, carried away by the arguments
of convenience and comfort, will even give you credit
for depth of thinking and lofty spirituality.

But try only to engage in constructive work,
make the slightest attempt towards leading your
flock in the path of positive Judaism, and you will
find out soon enough how great the obstacles you will
have to conquer, and how feeble your efforts to remove
them. There you will accomplish nothing without
that quality of יראת שמים, "fear of God," begotten
by that realization of the Divine Presence which
makes the Rabbi not only a נאה דורש a "beautiful
expounder of the Law," but also a נאה מקיים, a
"beautiful observer of the law," which eliminates all
self and makes of man a real servant of the Lord,
ready for all sacrifice and rejoicing in it. To take
one or two concrete cases: We are all deploring the
decay of the Sabbath; we constantly preach against
it and sit in conclave trying to ward off the danger
to Judaism resulting from this desecration. But I
tell you frankly that the Rabbi who will use his
freedom of interpretation to explain the laws regarding
the Sabbath in such a way that they should not interfere with his own pleasures and comforts, has no
right to admonish his flock not to make use of the
same freedom of interpretation so as to evade the
laws which interfere with their daily bread. The first
thing the Rabbi has to do is to keep the Sabbath
himself. Again, we constantly bewail the disappear-

ance of the Jewish home, but the Rabbi who removes all Jewish symbols from his house, and ignores all the institutions making for Jewish life, is not the man to arrest in any way the decay of Judaism, which he is so deeply bemoaning. The first thing he will have to do is to have a strictly Jewish home himself. This is especially the case with the share the Rabbi is expected to take in social questions. Nothing is easier than to denounce others and to "accelerate" public opinion. The role of the agitator is played to perfection easily enough. The morning papers and the very gossip of the street furnish you with sufficient materials. But as long as the Rabbi himself is not free from all worldly ambition, from all the vices of hunting after power and cheap popularity, his words will not have the slightest effect. He becomes in such cases a mere actor for the time being, without any real concern in the tragedy which he conjures up and impersonates.

It is recorded that when a Rabbi once asked his colleague why miracles happened so frequently in olden times and occur so rarely now, the answer he received was that it was different with the men of yore, who gave up their lives for the Sanctification of the Name. Now, take the history of the world, search the annals of our race, and see for yourself whether this greatest of all miracles, the conversion of a community to righteousness, or even the regeneration of a single individual, was ever effected by oratory alone, or rather by the saintly men who sacrificed, as just indicated, their very lives in the service of ideas and ideals.

The fact is, we are again in need of the sprinkling cf saints which alone possesses the secret of saving humanity. I had occasion once to quote the saying of our ancient sages that when the Holy One, blessed be He, saw that the righteous were to be few, He planted, or distributed them over the various generations. The righteous are apparently so few that even Providence has to be economical in their use. Nor are they of the noisy or boisterous kind. The description given of them is: Their life is even like that of Moses, a continuous mourning for the glory of God and the glory of Israel, at present obscured; a perpetual longing for Israel's salvation, whilst their activity forms one long effort towards making peace between heaven and earth. They are, again, exceedingly meek and gentle, never claiming thanks for themselves. They come and go without creating any disturbance, and they are exceedingly devoted to the study of the Torah.

Indeed, there is a certain delicacy about the whole composition of the saint which would make him rather timid, retired within himself, and shrinking back from contact with the many. Yet, somehow, his person becomes the centre of all beneficial activities. Solemn, severe and even distant as he may occasionally appear, his love of God and his love of man is sure to attract without any visible effort on his part, the best and the purest among us. But even the less pure element of society, nay, even the decadent and degenerate, will only dread them, but they will never hate them. Even the most abandoned can never quite forget their heavenly descent so as to disassociate themselves entirely from their pristine and native state and hate the angels. The only misfortune ·is that the evil one, as somebody put it, aware of this weakness of ours for our original heavenly connection, manages to appear in the disguise of an innocent cherub.

Of supreme importance is the saint's devotion to the study of the Law. The old maxim ascribed to Hillel, the meekest of men, "no ignorant person can be a saint or truly pious," remains true notwithstanding the holy terror felt at it by a certain class of theologians. Indeed, learning is the only safeguard against the just-mentioned sham cherubs. Piety without learning is apt, as is shown by the history of so many sects, to degenerate into mere ranting, making religion a caricature of itself. Least of all is ignorance compatible with the office of the Jewish minister, standing in the service of the Synagogue, which from its very appearance on the stage of history, proclaimed the study of the Torah as one of its three essential institutions. It would not even injure the Rabbi if he should from time to time engage in some scientific work, publishing occasionally a learned article on some historical topic, or even editing some ancient Hebrew text—in spite of the glorious discovery made recently that Isaiah never indulged in such vanities as a Doctor's Thesis, and that Amos never wrote a commentary—not even to his own prophecies. By the way, I wish he would have done so. It would have saved us a great deal of trouble, and I believe a greater deal of Higher Criticism. The author of the Book of Enoch tells us that, "it was not

intended when man was created that he should give
confirmation to his good faith with pen and ink and
such wise." This is angelic indeed, but humanly
speaking, it *was* intended when learned institutions
were created, that their graduates should, by some
scientific work, give confirmation of their continuing
the studies in which they were initiated by their
alma mater.

Of more consequence even to the Rabbi is the
Law-mindedness, or Law-conscience, which he will
acquire by his devotion to the study of the Torah, in
which the legal element is so strongly represented. It
is only, as I believe, by such a Law-conscience that
the world will profit most by the advice and counsel
of the Rabbi. I must explain a little more clearly.
During the recent controversy regarding the anti-race-
track bills before the Legislature, remarks were made
in the press to the effect that such laws as designed by
the Governor (Hughes) had an "Oriental" air about
them. I have not the paper before me, but as far
as I can remember, the drift of the remark was that
such legislation is an infringement of Christian
liberty, and that the whole tendency to regulate conduct by legislation is a characteristic of Oriental
despotism, incompatible with the notion of human
dignity and self-government, as understood by the
Occidental man.

Now, it is not my intention to enter here upon
the question of Orientalism and Occidentalism. The
Occidental man seems to have entirely forgotten that
he is under indebtedness for certain spiritual pos-

sessions to his brother of the Sunrise; which he cannot
repay—not even with smokeless powder or long-range
guns. Nor is it necessary for me to dwell on the merits
of this particular law now under consideration. Indeed, with the Jew, it will in no way bear discussion.
The Jew has no other name for gambling than the
old Scriptural expression, תועבת ה' "abomination to
the Lord." What concerns us here is the underlying
principle of Law, which divided us from the rest of
the world for more than eighteen centuries. What I
wish to impress upon you is that it is this conception
of law, of the necessity of law in the divine economy
of the universe, of the binding authority of law and
the absolute sovereignty and grace of law, that
Judaism is pre-eminently fitted to assert and to establish. Against this stronghold, the desperate assaults
of the centuries and of the creeds of the world have
dashed in vain. It is this tendency, hostile to the
principle of authority, Law and obedience, which it
will be your mission to combat. There are objects
which God hates, and there are objects which God
loves, and these objects are to the Jew formulated
into commandments, prohibitive on the one side, and
affirmative on the other, demanding implicit obedience.
God is not a mere figurehead. He not only reigns,
but governs. Everywhere—in the temple, in the
judge's seat, in the family, in the farm, and in the
market place—His Presence is felt in enforcing the
laws bearing His *imprimatur*, "I am the Lord, thy
God." Ethical monotheism is a splendid phrase.
Monotheism is good, but God is better. For mono-

theism savors somewhat of the abstract, of the mere idea, a vague tendency, subject to what we are pleased to call our freedom of interpretation. With the Jew, God is the only reality, or, as our sublime liturgy has it,

חי וקים נורא ומרום וקדוש

"A living and enduring terrible and exalted and holy God." Ethics are good, but laws and commandments, bidden and commanded by God, are better; and all such phrases as idealism, spirituality and religiosity will avail nothing as long as you omit to urge the great principle that the Holy One of Israel, "in His Holiness, gave law unto His people." Our Torah proclaimed the love of God with heart and soul and might, and the world accepted it as the consummation of its purpose. It taught the love of neighbor as oneself, and the world appropriated it as an original inspiration; but together with this Israel proclaimed the love of law. Psalmist and prophet add the law of love. "I hate vain thoughts, but Thy law I love," sings the Psalmist (Psalm 119:113), and it is through this love and adherence to law that the love of God and the love of fellowman is made effective. To urge this upon your community in all its force and all its significance seems to me the mission of the Rabbi of the present generation. And it is only by representing this principle of law and authority and obedience that Judaism can again become a factor in the conversion of the world.

LECTOR MEIR FRIEDMANN.*

IN THE death of Lector M. Friedmann, or as he preferably signed himself in his Hebrew works, Meir Ish Shalom (Meir, Man of Peace), Judaism has sustained an irreparable loss. The oft-quoted exclamation of an ancient Rabbi at the decease of his colleague, "When the scholar or Talmud Chacham dies, who can furnish us with his substitute?" could nowhere be applied with more force than to the death which Israel is now mourning. Friedmann has no substitute; he cannot be replaced. For, this was the main characteristic of the man, that he never reminded you of anyone else but himself. No school can claim him; no party was strong enough to force on him its label, though he came in touch with all schools and all parties. He always remained, Meir Ish Shalom.

This independence may have been largely due to the peculiar story of his youth. Briefly stated, it is this. Friedmann was born in 1831 in the village of Kraszna, district of Kashau, Hungary. Till twelve years of age he remained in this village, where he received his first instruction in the Talmud. He then continued his studies in the Yeshiboth, or higher Talmudical colleges, for which Hungary was distinguished at that period. Of particular importance was the college at Unguar, where he studied under the supervision of Rabbi Meir Eisenstadt, who was

*Paper contributed to the *American Hebrew*, December 11, 1908.

a distant relative of his mother. There, to use a
Talmudic expression, he saw the first sign of blessing
in his studies, but became also, through the influence
of Eisenstadt, attached to the teachings of the
mystics and the Chasidim, and spent a good deal of
his time in fasting and other ascetic practices. At
that time he also thought of emigrating to Palestine.
The Revolution of 1848, however, prevented him from
carrying out his favorite plan. At the age of sixteen
or seventeen he turned his attention to the Bible,
studying it with the aid of the German translation
and commentaries of Mendelssohn and his school.
The *Shire Tifereth* (a sort of Mosaide) of Wessely
became his great model for Hebrew style. At the
age of twenty he settled in Miskolcz, where he received
his first instruction in the German language, as well
as in geography from Michael Heilprin, perhaps the
same Heilprin who afterwards emigrated to this
country, in which he became so famous. His Rabbinic
diploma, of which, however, he never made any
use, preferring to settle down as a farmer, he obtained
at the age of twenty-four. A great sorrow befell him
soon, which made him leave Hungary and emigrate
to Vienna, where he arrived in the year 1858. There
he attended lectures at the University, but was about
the same time appointed Lector in Bible and various
Rabbinic studies in the Beth Hamidrash, in which
capacity he was active until his death. He also
occupied the same chair in the *Israelitisch Theologische
Lehranstalt*, of Vienna, which was afterwards founded.

His education was that of an autodidact, and the
influences reaching into his life of the most contra-

dictory tendencies. But what would have led in any other man of a less marked individuality to dilettantism and shallowness in his studies and to deformity in his character, blended in Friedmann to a harmonious whole and developed a personality of unique charm and originality. The Yeshiba and University gave him erudition and method; whilst his contact with Chasidism and his life as a farmer provided him with a touch of saintliness and simplicity, which became marked features of his nature.

This is not the place for an appreciation of Lector Friedmann's scientific work. He made his first debut with his edition of the Sifre in 1864. Hardly a year has passed since then in which he did not enrich Jewish literature by one contribution or another, extending over all its departments, Bible criticism included. Friedmann's various essays in the periodical *Beth Talmud*, on the order of the Pentateuch and on the story of the patriarchs, as well as his commentary on Samuel and Judges, should be read by everyone who would learn what a *Jewish liberal* Bible criticism means. Only a few months ago he published an old Rabbinic text, *Baraitha d' Melecheth Hammishkan*, with a critical commentary and introduction. Death itself found him active in the edition of a critical text of the *Torath Kohanim*, of which he sent me several sheets already printed off. Suffice to remark, that he was the pioneer in the art of critical editions of Rabbinic texts, and that all his publications became a model in this respect for other workers in the same field. His edition of the Mechilta in particular formed an epoch in Rabbinical exegesis,

for it not only gave us the first scientific edition of
an ancient Rabbinic text, in which the Halachah is
nearly as strongly represented as the Hagada, but
in the Introduction it also revealed to us the possibilities of this ancient Midrashic literature, and its
bearing upon the exegesis of the Bible. It was also
in this Introduction that Friedmann maintained
that there existed another Mechilta composed in the
schools of Rabbi Simon ben Yochai, a forecast which
was afterwards amply verified by the importation of
Yemen MSS. and various discoveries in the Genizah.

Great, however, as he was a scholar, he was even
greater as a Jew and a man.   Notwithstanding his
strict scientific methods, which demanded from him
absolute obedience to method and precision, he could
never sink his own personality to the level which turns
learning into mere manual work, keeping your note
books in good order and putting your references in
their proper places, or what some savant called,
"Zettelgelehrsamkeit."   And whilst he endeavored
to elucidate the text under discussion, he would also
seek to widen your horizon in matters not strictly
connected with the subject in hand.   In the labyrinth
of all references and cross-references to parallel passages, textual emendations and verbal explanations,
we are often struck by a sudden remark, introduced
usually by the words, "Thus says Meir, Man of
Peace," transferring us into quite another region,
history, Bible criticism or theology.

Nor would he ever allow you to forget that besides
using your brain as a thinking machine, you are also
possessed of a living soul, and that soul, a Jewish

soul, to which he considered it his duty and his
privilege to address himself. And thus the sudden
flashes just indicated would assume occasionally a
spiritual character, something between a prayer and
a promise; as for instance, in his notes to the *Pesikta
Rabbati*, where at the end of a long disquisition as
to the original arrangement of his texts, he suddenly exclaims:

"Be not frightened at the aping religions, for
behold, all that the prophets said and what the wise
men have told relates to Israel, not to any other nation. And as long as their words were not realized
in us, the sons of Abraham, Isaac and Jacob, they
cannot be regarded as fulfilled. Blessed be he who hopes
and will see the days when Edom shall be a possession
and Israel shall do valiantly."

The "aping religions" are Christianity and Mo-
hammedanism, a term used sometimes by Spanish
philosophers, which Friedmann was fond of repeating.
His admirable introduction, again, to the *Seder
Eliahu*, forming the best essay in existence on the
Elijah legend in Hebrew literature is, at the same
time, a long learned epic, giving the story of Israel's
aspirations both as a religion revealed in its Torah,
and as a nation manifest in its eschatology. Occasionally, he also seizes the opportunity to warn against
assimilation. This is especially the tendency traceable in his monograph on the twentieth chapter of
Ezekiel, which he published twenty years ago.
"What the elders of Israel who consulted Ezekiel
wanted," he says in effect, "was to build themselves
a Temple in Babylon, centralizing there the Jewish

worship to be performed by priests or first-born, and thus establish there a minor sanctuary in the midst of Babylon (as a substitute for the Temple in Jerusalem). But it was against this which the prophet protested so vehemently, for such a sanctuary would lead to abandoning all thought of returning to the Holy Land, which must end in absorption by the surrounding nations, whose deeds they will imitate, so that the name of God will be profaned; whilst the real destiny of Israel was the perfection of the nation, so that they be a separate nation in a separate country, with God as their King."

Entertaining such sentiments, (though there are passages in his writings which would be considered rank heresy by the common nationalist,) it is not to be wondered at that he was one of the first Jewish scholars who approved of the Zionistic movement. Whether he ever was an active member of any Zionistic organization, I am unable to say; but he certainly sympathized with the movement, defending it both in his private conversation and letters to his friends and in public. I am especially thinking of a short article of his in *The Hashiloach*, where he quotes one of our mediaeval authorities who maintained that the redemption which Israel is expecting now need not necessarily be accompanied by the interference with the laws of nature as that from Egypt was, but may also be accomplished without the intervention of miracles. He further quotes, in this connection, the well-known passage from the Midrash, that God's blessing does not relieve man from his share of activity and effort: and proceeds to say, "This is answer enough to those in Israel who oppose the great movement in our day, which, if the whole nation should unite to aid in it, would soon bring about the fulfilment of the Scriptural promise, 'That the Lord thy God may bless thee in all the work of thine hand which thou doest!' "

"The conversation of the men of the Holy Land," says the Midrash, "is a Torah in itself," and so was that of Friedmann,—instructive and suggestive. The old adage, *"Olam keminhago noheg"* (the world moves on its customary lines) was one of his favorite sayings; and in his simplicity of character, there was nothing farther from him than the wish to appear soaring above the world. I remember to have read the statement of some Zadik that simplicity should be the only object of prayer by man, and I knew many who constantly prayed for it, but the more they prayed the more self-conscious they became. To Friedmann, this gift was granted without a prayer. All through life he never assumed the role of the "winner of souls," though his influence has reached more men and women than that of many an official "leader of the generation." Even towards his pupils he never asserted the role of master. He treated them as friends and comrades, mingling in their conversations and pastimes. Yet Friedmann could never be commonplace, even if he wished to be; and in his talk there would always be some striking remark, which could only be described as a flash of genius. It must now be more than thirty years since several young men were gathered in his private room attached to the Beth Hamidrash, engaged in easy talk, when the conversation took a serious character, turning upon the old problem of the destiny of Israel. Those were the times when the idea of the Mission, with its necessary consequence of Israel's final absorption in the great sea of the nations, was regarded as an indisputable dogma; and so it was declared to be by the majority of those present. Whereupon Friedmann suddenly exclaimed, "Gentlemen, this is frog theology, and unworthy of a human being!" After much guessing as to the meaning of his words, it was afterwards found that he was referring to a certain story, which may be paraphrased somewhat in the following way: A frog challenged the accomplishment of David as a singer in Israel, maintaining that its incessant croaking has a much sweeter sound, and further alleging that it represents the martyr animal of creation, as it never hesitates to swim in the current carrying it to the abode of the sea-monsters, to be ultimately swallowed up by a Leviathan exclusively dependent for its sustenance on frog food. By this, the frog asserted that its death accomplished the message of its Maker. No "mission talk" of this kind was ever heard again in this circle. And let there be no mistake about it. Friedmann was by no means what is called "orthodox." He gave evidence of this both in his writings and conversation. There is the famous rebuke by him administered to a certain extremist, "I have seen many a man wrapped up in his *Tallith* and *Tefillin*, but harboring a non-Jewish soul, and I am addressing myself only to Jewish souls." Indeed, if anything could have provoked his wrath, it was fanaticism and persecution, in which at those times the orthodox used to indulge more than their opponents,—which conditions I may remark *en passant* have been reversed nowadays, when the "opponents" have the majority and feel strong enough for this blessed task. But Friedmann hated empty phrases of all kinds, while he would never allow to pass unchallenged any stigma upon Israel—which was his grand passion. It was in this way that he saved many a young man both from scoffing at the *Haskalah* and from the cheap platitudes of the rationalism so rampant in the seventies.

What I owe him personally concerns the world very little, nor have I the words at my command to express adequately what he meant to me as a teacher and friend for nearly forty years. Our ancient sages say, "When one of a band (of friends) dies, let all the surviving members feel troubled." The trouble is not so much a consequence of fear at the approach of one's own end, as the fact that by the loss of parents and relatives and the dropping away of intimate friends, life becomes constantly poorer in all that makes life valuable and desirable. And nothing remains but to live on memories, cherishing the memory of this Prince in the Torah and this great Man of Peace.

ABRAHAM LINCOLN.*

A LEXANDER H. Stephens, in his characterization of Lincoln, says, "The Union with him in
sentiment rose to the sublimity of a religious mysticism; whilst his ideas of its structure and formation
in logic rested upon nothing but the subtleties of
a sophism."

Stephens was, by agreement of all, the ablest
historian of the Confederacy, and, some think, its
greatest man; and those who read his argument for
the Union contained in his address given at Milledge-
ville, Georgia, before the War between the States
began, will further admit that he had the gift of seeing below the surface of things, for the condition of
affairs as seen then by superficial observers was all
in favor of secession. Stephens was also one of the
few prominent men of the Thirtieth Congress for
whom Lincoln conceived great admiration during
his first appearance at Washington in the capacity
of a member of the House of Representatives. Lincoln was present when Stephens delivered "the best
speech of an hour's length" he had ever heard, which
moved him so deeply that his "old, withered eyes
were full of tears." At a later date, again, when Lincoln stood before the country as the President-elect,
Stephens was, perhaps, the only Southern statesman

---

*Lecture delivered on the Occasion of Lincoln's Hundreth Anni-
versary, at the Jewish Theological Seminary, February
11, 1909.

whose opinion Lincoln solicited in reference to the coming struggle. Some historians maintain that Lincoln seriously considered the advisability of inviting Stephens to become a member of his cabinet. A characterization of Lincoln coming from such a source is worthy of our attention. It will, therefore, not be amiss if we devote this hour to this trait of religious mysticism in his character, touching also on one or two other traits which, by their seeming contrast, served either as a corrective or as an emphasis of this mystical trait.

Whether this aspect has ever been the subject of special treatment by any other writer, I am unable to say. The list of Lincolniana prepared by the Library of Congress and consisting mostly of writings relating to Lincoln, covers a large quarto volume of eighty-six pages. This list was published in 1906, and we may assume that the last two years have brought us a new harvest of Lincolniana. There you will find Lincoln as a lawyer, Lincoln as an organizer, Lincoln as an orator, Lincoln as a general, Lincoln as a debater, Lincoln as a master of men, Lincoln as a financier, and ever so many more Lincolns. For all I know, or rather do not know, the possibility is not excluded that in this enormous mass of literature, Lincoln may have also been treated from the point of view I intend to approach him this evening. Even in this case, it may perhaps not be entirely uninteresting to listen to one whose first acquaintance with Lincoln was made in far-distant Roumania through the medium of Hebrew newspapers some forty-five years ago. There Lincoln was described as originally a wood-chopper (prose for "rail-splitter"), which so fired the imagination of the lad as to recognize in the President of the United States, a new Hillel, for legend described the latter as having been engaged in the same occupation before he was called by the people to the dignity of Patriarch, or President of the Sanhedrin. Years have come and years have gone, and the imagination of the boy was in many respects corrected by the reading of serious books bearing on the history of the United States, and particularly on that of the Civil War. But this in no way diminished his admiration for his hero, Abraham Lincoln, whom he was always studying, from the viewpoint of the student of Jewish literature; a literature which, in spite of its eastern origin, affords so much in the way of parallel and simile to the elucidation of the great Western of the Westerns.

The youth of Lincoln offered little or no opportunity for the display of religious mysticism. Some historians of the high and dry kind take, as it seems, a genuine pleasure in speaking of the surroundings that were about Lincoln as "coarse, ignorant and poverty-stricken." In a certain measure this is true. Lincoln himself described the part of Indiana in which he grew up as a "wild region, with many bears and other animals still in the woods." The conditions were thus semi-barbaric, and may be held responsible for whatever of coarseness and uncouthness respectability detected in the life of Lincoln. Barbaric conditions, however, have the great redeeming virtue that there is little room in them for vulgarity, and this compensates for the lack of many

an accomplishment of civilization. By "vulgarity,"
I mean that vice of civilization which makes man
ashamed of himself and his next of kin, and pretend
to be somebody else. It is a kind of social hypocrisy,
and not less pernicious to the development of character than religious hypocrisy to the development
of saintliness. With Lincoln in particular, such
simulation to which we are broken in, consciously or
unconsciously, in a great civilized community, would
have proven fatal, as his great strength lay in the fact
that he always remained himself, or, as one of his
eulogists aptly said: "Lincoln is not a type. He
stands alone—no ancestors, no fellows, no successors."

More serious, perhaps, is the charge of ignorance.
In the biography for the Directory of Congress,
Lincoln gave himself the mark, "education defective."
Learned institutions of any kind were almost unknown in those regions. "If a straggler supposed to
understand Latin happened to sojourn in the neighborhood, he was looked upon as a wizard." But even
books, which have wrought so many miracles in pav-
ing the way for many a self-taught man, leading to
the highest academic honors, were scarce. The whole
settlement in which Lincoln spent the greatest part
of his early youth, could hardly have commanded
such a library as any youngster in our days, even
among the poorer classes, might look upon as his
property on the day of his confirmation. Even the
itinerant ministers of religion who would occasionally
visit these pioneer settlements were less distinguished
for their sources of information than for their forcible
language, well spiced with brimstone and other

nether-world ingredients. But, as has already been pointed out by several biographers of Lincoln, there is no cause to remonstrate with Providence on this account. For the few books which Lincoln might regard as his own, so that he could pore over them day and night, were of the best kind, being the Bible, *Aesop's Fables*, *Robinson Crusoe*, *Pilgrim's Progress* and Weems' *Life of Washington*." All these works left a permanent impression upon him, which is traceable in the simplicity of his lucid style, and in his love of fable and parable as a means of illustrating a point. Shakespeare and a few other English poets with whom he made acquaintance at a somewhat later date, may be added to this list. Perhaps it would have been better for Lincoln's reputation if Lincoln's youth, which brought him to Illinois, where he came in contact with a more advanced civilization, would in respect of book learning, have not gone much further beyond the books or kind of books just mentioned—in addition, of course, to such works on the history and the Constitution of the United States, as were necessary for his mental equipment in his future career as lawyer and states-man. For those were the days in which Volney's *Ruins* and Tom Paine's *Age of Reason* were taken as seriously and read with as much eagerness as a certain class of books dabbling in evolution and the survival of the fittest—pulpit evolution, we might term it—are read and discussed today. Lincoln in his zeal for knowledge did not escape the tendency of his age, and in impulsive moments gave expression to certain rationalistic views which were afterwards seized upon with much avidity by friend and foe as representing "the true Lincoln." The student of Hebrew literature, when reading such "Lincolns," emphasizing the shortcomings of his youth and the lack of presentable ancestry, involuntarily thinks of the ancient Rabbinic but truly democratic principle: "They appoint not a leader over the community unless there hangs a mass of reptiles (in the shape of certain blemishes) behind him, lest he become overbearing." Some writers apparently mistake the reptiles for an essential part of the man.

Lincoln outgrew all his puerile rationalistic performances soon enough when the time for such action came as could never have been accomplished without faith, in all its sublimity. This action was the saving of the Union, which was at the same time the great opportunity of his life, and unfortunately also the occasion of his death. No religious hero ever entered upon his mission to conquer the world for an idea or creed with more reverence and a deeper feeling of the need of divine assistance than did Lincoln, when he was about to leave his home and his old associates and associations, good and evil, for his new home and his new life in Washington. "I now leave," he said in his farewell address to his fellow citizens at Springfield, Illinois, "not knowing when or whether I may return, with a task before me greater than that which rested upon Washington. Without the assistance of that Divine Being who ever attended him, I cannot succeed. With that assistance, I cannot fail. Trusting in Him who can go with me, and remain with you, and be everywhere for good, let us con-

fidently hope that all will yet be well." This sounds
like a prayer; but the concluding line of his Inaugural, given in Washington on the 4th of March,
1861, rise to the heights of a mystical hymn.

"We are not enemies, but friends. We must not
be enemies. Though passion may have strained, it
must not break our bonds of affection. The mystic
cords of memory, stretching from every battlefield
and patriot grave to every living heart and hearth-
stone all over this broad land, will yet swell the
chorus of the Union when again touched, as surely
they will be, by the better angels of our nature."

"Higher criticism" attributes these lines to a
suggestion of Seward, but it was Lincoln, as admitted
even by the "higher critics," who gave them life and
spirit and who transformed them into an illustration
of perfect and tender beauty.

The expression, "mystic chords *of memory*," is
significant. Napoleon the Great is recorded to have
once made the apt remark, "Religion means memory."
If the Union was to be saved, it had to be raised to
the dignity of a religion, which means memory, an
object hallowed by past associations, which alone
holds out promises for the future. Notwithstanding
all realistic conceptions of history, the "better angels
of our nature" that alone terminate great issues by
their readiness for sacrifice, will never enlist in a cause
purely material. The better angels fought for the
shrine of their gods; for the expansion of a religious
idea of which they were possessed; for their existence
as a nation—that is, their institutions, their language,
their literature, their traditional customs and usages;

for glory and honor—in brief, for their memories;
though gold and other material gains always proved
a valuable auxiliary as attracting the minor angels.
In the case of America, the Western man might
struggle for an outlet to the Gulf, the Eastern man
might contend for the protection of infant industries,
but to engage in a war of such dimensions as the
Civil War was, with its loss of men and loss of treasure, the *dynamis* of an idea and ideal was indispensable. And this idea, defined by the word "Union," was to all intents and purposes a mystical one,
as every religious idea is. The State, reaching
directly into the life of the citizen through the means
of its courts, its schools and its powers of direct
taxation, was something concrete and tangible,
evident to the dullest intellect in its distribution of
reward and punishment, and realized as the tutelar
deity of the community. On the other hand, the
benefits of the Central Government were, as Stephens
rightly pointed out, so silent and unseen, that they
were seldom thought of or appreciated, just as is the
oxygen in the air we breathe little thought of or
appreciated, although it is the very element that gives
us life and strength. Hence, the Union was a mere
abstraction, invisible, an hypostasis of memory and
hope, and appealing only to our sense of reverence
and worship or "the better angels of our nature."

The realization of great ideas, heaven-conceived
and earth-born, is not accomplished without travail
and woe, deep sorrow and repeated disappointment.
History of things past, and apocalyptic pictures of
events to come, furnish sufficient proof of this. And

such was the case with the idea of the Union before it could pass into the consciousness of the people as a solemn fact. The effect of the first Union defeats upon the great persons of Washington and their entourage is recorded by Walt Whitman as "a mixture of awful consternation, uncertainty, rage, shame, helplessness and stupefying disappointment." Lincoln himself was no exception in this respect, though his calm disposition preserved him from "rage." His sublime faith, again, in the cause of the Union which, in the manner of a Luther at the Diet of Worms, he considered to be God's cause, made real despair impossible. But this confidence did not exclude moments of terrible anguish and intense suffering. At times of frightful suspense, he would envy the common soldier, and would willingly have exchanged places with him, whilst after the terrible defeat of the Union forces at Fredericksburg, he exclaimed: "Oh, if there is a man out of hell that suffers more than I do, I pity him!" His normal condition may be described as expectation inspired by the sense of the awful. It is well depicted in the answer given by him to a delegation of ministers importuning him with their well-meant counsel; and probably reflects his own mental attitude: "Gentlemen," he said, "suppose all the property you possess were in gold, and you had placed it in the hands of Blondin to carry across the Niagara River on a rope. With slow, cautious, steady steps he walks the rope, bearing your all. Would you shake the cable and keep shouting to him, 'Blondin, stand up a little straighter! Blondin, stoop a little more; go a little

faster; lean more to the south! Now lean a little
more to the north!' Would that be your behaviour
in such an emergency? No! You would hold your
breath, everyone of you, as well as your tongues.
You would keep your hands off until he was safe
on the other side." This simile is rather homely in
its local color, but it struck me as peculiarly forcible
many years ago, long before I had ever seen Niagara
Falls or ever heard of Blondin and his performances.
It somehow sounded to me like an echo from the
following passage to be found in Bedresi's *Examination of the World*, that may be paraphrased thus:
"The World is a stormy sea, of depth immeasurable
and expanse unbounded. Time is a frail bridge built
over it. The one end is fastened by cords to the
Vast that precedes existence, and its terminus gives
glimpses of eternal glory through the light of the
presence of the King. The width of the bridge is
as a man's cubit, and the rails have disappeared.
But thou, Son of Man, without thy consent, thou
livest and continuously dost progress over it from
the day of thy birth. When thou meditatest upon
the narrowness of the span, having no side path
either to the right or to the left, when thou perceivest
death and destruction encompassing thee as a wall
on either side, will not thy heart fail, and wilt thou
still glory in power and fame?" Bedresi flourished
in the thirteenth century, and his book was written
in Hebrew, and I hardly need say that Lincoln never
as much as even heard of it.

With the consciousness of the Union, or the body-
politic, there developed in Lincoln also the conscious-

ness of the national sin, and the need of confession,
which indeed is another manifestation of religious
mysticism. Renan, in his famous review of Amiel's
Journal, remarks: "He (Amiel) speaks of sin, of
salvation, etc., as though they were realities. Sin in
particular, engrosses his attention and saddens him."
Sin was also a reality with Lincoln, weighing heavily
on his conscience, not to be countenanced on any
aesthetic considerations or argued away by any philosophic or sociological formula. There it was, and it
cried for atonement. Thus, in one of his proclamations, he addresses the nation in the following words:
"We have grown in numbers, wealth and power as no
other nation has ever grown; but we have forgotten
God. . . . . We have been the recipients of the
choicest bounties of heaven. Intoxicated by unbroken
success, we have become . . . too proud to pray
to the God that made us. We have been preserved
these many years in peace and prosperity. It behooves
us, then, ... to confess our national sins,
and to pray for clemency and forgiveness." The
plural "we" in these proclamations is to be taken
literally to include the North, whom he by no means
acquitted of the great national sin. "If God wills,"
he wrote once, "the removal of a great wrong, and
wills also that we of the North, as well as you of the
South, shall pay fairly for our complicity in that
wrong, impartial history will find therein new cause
to attest and revere the justice and goodness of God."
And in the nation he included fully his own person.
He is even said to have exclaimed once in a moment
of deep depression, "If our American society and the

United States Government are demoralized and overthrown, it will come from the voracious desire for office, this wriggle to live without toil, work and labor, from which I am not free myself."

The greatest human and at the same time religious document, however, left us by Lincoln, for which history hardly affords any model, except perhaps that of the Scriptures is, as is well known, his Second Inaugural: " 'The Almighty has His own purpose. Woe unto the world because of offense; for it must needs be that offenses come; but woe to that man by whom the offense cometh.' If we shall suppose that American slavery is one of those offenses which, in the providence of God must needs come, but which, having continued through His appointed time, He now wills to remove, and that He gives to both North and South this terrible war as the woe due to those by whom the offense came, shall we discern therein any departure from the divine attributes which the believers in a living God always ascribe to him? Fondly do we hope—fervently do we pray— that this mighty scourge of war may speedily pass away. Yet, if God wills that it continue until all the wealth piled by the bondsman's two hundred and fifty years of unrequited toil shall be sunk, and until every drop of blood drawn with the lash shall be paid by another drawn with the sword, as was said three thousand years ago, so still it must be said: 'The judgments of the Lord are true and righteous altogether.' "

When reading these lines just given, one can scarcely believe that they formed a part of a message

addressed in the nineteenth century to an assembly
composed largely of men of affairs and representatives
of a special political party, surrounded by all the
pomp and paraphernalia of one of the greatest
legislative bodies the world has ever seen. One
rather imagines himself transported into a camp of
contrite sinners determined to leave the world and its
vanities behind them, possessed of no other thought
but that of reconciliation with their God, and addressed by their leader when about to set out on a
course of penance. Indeed, how little the religious
sentiments manifest in this document echoed those
of either party is evident from a letter of Lincoln to
Thurlow Weed, with reference to the Second Inaugural: ". . . . I believe it is not immediately
popular. Men are not flattered by being shown that
there has been a difference of purpose between the
Almighty and them. To deny it, however, in this
case, is to deny that there is a God governing the
world. It is a truth which I thought needed to be
told, and, as whatever of humiliation there is in it
falls most directly on myself, I thought others might
afford for me to tell it." To take upon one's self
the burden of humiliation in which the whole nation
should share, is another feature of religious mysticism
which so vividly realizes in the sphere of morality
the unity of humanity, and in the realm of history the
union of the nation, so that it does not hesitate to
suffer and to atone for the sins of the generation.

Religious mysticism, however, has the defects of
its quality, and the defects are very serious. For,
the superabundance of zeal and extravagant enthu-

siasm such as often accompany religious mysticism may, as experience teaches, very easily degenerate into fanaticism and lawlessness, brushing aside all legal restraints and occasionally ignoring even all humane considerations. From these dangers, Lincoln was preserved by his legal training and not less by his divine humor.

Many writers have shown what Lincoln's experience at the bar meant for him in his later historic guidance of the nation. But the best gift these twenty-three years in the legal profession brought him was that it created in him a legal conscience, which proved immune against the possible excesses of mysticism. He certainly considered slavery as *the* sin, par excellence. "If slavery is not wrong, nothing is wrong," and to this conviction of the wrong of slavery, statements may be quoted dating from his earliest manhood. About this fact all the best authorities are agreed now, whatever doubts there may have been expressed concerning it a generation ago, and there is no necessity to adduce here more proofs. But he was equally convinced of the supremacy of the law, as embodied in the Constitution, its authorized interpretations, and the enactments made under its provisions. Liberty is sacred, but so is the Constitution, the sacred writ of the United States, and in opposition to the most distinguished of his colleagues, he was loath to agree that it can be ruled out of court by the "higher law," or the "unwritten law." "Let every American," he exclaimed in one of his earlier speeches, "every lover of liberty, every well-wisher

to his posterity, swear by the blood of the Revolution
never to violate in the least particular the laws of
the country, and never to tolerate their violation
by others." Indeed, he considered "the increasing
disregard of the law which pervaded the country
as something of ill omen—the growing disposition
to substitute the wild and curious passions in lieu
of the sober judgments of the courts, and the worse
than savage mobs for the executive ministers of
justice." The passages just quoted are taken from
an address given by Lincoln in January, 1837, when
he was fully engaged in his profession as a lawyer.
But this conviction of the sovereignty of the law,
grows upon him with the growth of his personality
and the growth of the temptation to break it. He
is "naturally anti-slavery," as he expressed it, and is
the more on his guard not to follow the bent of his
nature. And the temptation was great indeed, when
we consider not only his own inclination, but the general
tendency of several of the leaders of his own party,
to think lightly of the Constitution, a tendency expressed in Stanton's well-known words: "It is
better to have a country without a Constitution than
a Constitution without a country." It is further
clear from Lincoln's famous letter to Hodges that
he shared to some degree in this feeling. Yet he
remained steadfast to his legal principles. He
admitted that there is such a thing as "bad laws,"
but the only remedy he saw was that they "should
be repealed as soon as possible; as long as they continue in force, they should be religiously observed."

Hence his well-known hesitation to emancipate the slave, and his recurring to it in the end only as a measure of war, which he thought justified by the Constitution.

This legal conscience found a powerful ally in Lincoln's humor. No flaw in an argument could elude it, no human weakness in either party could escape it, but it possessed also that divine quality of wounding and healing at the same time, which made it with no real malice to anyone and charitable in the end to others.

Nothing is more congenial to the student of Jewish literature than these ingredients in Lindoln's mental make-up which found their expression in his stories, his repartee, his wit and sarcasm, in all of which he was such a consummate master. In the literature of the Jew, the *Mashal* (comparison) or *Maaseh* (story) are the most prominent. They were mostly used by way of illustration. The use of the *Mashal* in particular, is illustrated by the Rabbis by another "mashal" comparing it to the handle which enables people to take hold of a thing or subject. Occasionally it forms the introduction to the most solemn discourse. Thus it is recorded of a famous Rabbi that before he commenced his lectures on points of law before his disciples, he would first tell them something humorous to make them laugh, and then, resuming his natural self, commenced in solemn frame of mind his discourse. I need hardly remind you here of the well-known tradition in connection with the President's first reading of the Emancipation Proclamation to the members of his cabinet (September 22, 1862). They met in his office at the White House, and then

took their seats in the usual order. Lincoln then took
Artemus Ward's book, and read from it the chapter,
"High-Handed Outrage at Utica," which he thought
very funny, and enjoyed the reading of it greatly,
while the members of the cabinet, except Stanton,
laughed with him. Then he fell into a grave tone and
began the discussion preceding the perusal of this
great historical and momentous document.

To give another example: Once when a Rabbi
wanted to impress his audience with the evil consequences of intemperance, he began: "Story: Once
upon a time there was a pious man whose father was
addicted to strong drink, which brought great shame
upon him. On one occasion, the pious man walked
in the street in a pouring rain, when he perceived a
drunken man lying in the gutter and exposed to the
abuse of the street urchins, who made sport of him.
He thereupon thought in his heart, 'I will induce
father to come here to show him the humiliation he
brings upon himself by his dissipation.' The father
came, but the first thing he did was to ask the drunken
man for the address of the inn where such good wine
was sold." This recalls to our mind Lincoln's well-
known answer to the charge brought against one of
his most successful generals that he sometimes drank
too much. Lincoln merely asked to know the brand
of whiskey consumed by him so that he "might
distribute it among some of the other generals."
Lincoln's pleading with his friends and foes that there
is no hope for Americans to live outside of the Constitution if they cannot any longer live in it (I am unable
to locate the passage or to give the exact words)
reminded me when I read it of the following Jewish

parable: ˙"Once upon a time, a fox was walking by
the banks of a river, and he saw the fish swimming
from place to place. 'Why this unrest?' asked the
fox. The fish answered, 'Because of the nets spread
out for us by the sons of men.' Thereupon the fox
said, 'Would you not prefer to move to the land and
I and you will live together, as my ancestors and yours
did before us?' The fish answered, 'Art thou the one
who is spoken of as the sage among the animals?
Thou art a fool. If, in our element of life we cannot
always escape danger, the less so in the element that
means death for us.' "

Lincoln's humor not only served him as a means of
instruction and illustration, but proved also an excellent weapon of offense and defence. You have all
probably heard the story which he told once when discussing the newspaper attacks on his administration,
emanating from the various quarters which agreed
in nothing except their hostility to the President:

"A traveler on the frontier found himself out of
his reckoning one night in a most inhospitable region.
A terrific thunderstorm came up, to add to his
trouble. He floundered along until at length his
horse gave out. The lightning afforded him the only
clue to his way, but the peals of thunder were frightful. One bolt, which seemed to crush the earth
beneath him, brought him to his knees. By no means
a praying man, his petition was short and to the point:
'O Lord, if it's all the same to you, give us a little
more light and a little less noise."

The noise indeed was terrific and light was necessary. I once read a remark that every great move-

ment is liable to suffer not less by the arrogance of
the few than by the ignorance of the many. The
many in this case were the people at large who, in
their slow and sluggish way, could be moved by the
sequence of events under the tuition of such a master
mind as Lincoln. More hopeless was the case of the
few who looked upon themselves as the elect, and
neither minded nor cared for the people behind them.
These self-constituted advisers did not take into
consideration that there were such things as a Constitution and Constitutional guarantees, which as
the sworn officer of the law Lincoln could not possibly
ignore. They were always ready with their counsel
to Lincoln, and even the logic of events never cured
them of their dogmatism and positiveness. Only
lately, I read a book by one of these elect, written
more than a generation after Lincoln's death, in
which the impression is conveyed that the Civil War
might have been easily averted had the President
but followed the advice offered to him by the writer
and his friends.

"And this reminds me of a story," to use a favorite
expression of Lincoln. I give the story in the peculiar version I heard it once from "one who tells"
(Maggid), though the main features of it are known
from the Midrashim and the Pseudepigrapha, not to
mention Milton's "Paradise Lost." "When the
Holy One, blessed be He, was about to create man,
He invited the angels and asked them for their
opinion. Their answer was, 'Let man not be created,
for he will prove a sinful creature.' And so indeed
it came to pass, 'that the wickedness of man was

upon the earth.' Then they came to God and said, 'We told you so!' The Lord's answer was, 'If you are so self-righteous, descend to the earth and see whether with all your heavenly bringing up you will turn out less proof against sin than man?' A certain number of angels did descend to earth, where they made the acquaintance of the daughters of man, 'and brought forth the generation of giants, men of renown.' But the great majority of the angels withdrew in a sullen mood to a remote corner of heaven, eternally absorbed in the admiration of their own virtue which prevented them from begetting giants and men of renown, and continuing out of sheer habit to sing the praise, not of God, but of themselves."

The counterpart of this celestial coterie is known on earth under various appellatives bestowed upon them by themselves, such as "illuminati," "elect," "seekers after perfection," etc., and the only way to meet them is with humor in its various aspects. Serious argument is of little use on such occasions, for they appeal to the will of God, "which prevails," and should be indeed the last appeal in all matters; but it never occurs to them that there is a possibility that they are not the chosen vessels for this revelation of the will of God. As Lincoln expressed it, "There is certainly no contending against the will of God, but still there is some difficulty in ascertaining and applying it to particular cases." How he dealt with the "certain ones" may be best illustrated by the following episode:

A member of a church, at a reception, closed his remarks with the pious hope "that the Lord is on our side." "I am not at all concerned about that," commented the President, "for we know that the Lord is always on the side of the right. But it is my constant anxiety and prayer that I and the nation should be on the Lord's side."

This suspicion against overzeal, which might make it possible for man not to be on the Lord's side even when in the service of a righteous cause, is one against which man has constantly to be on his guard. Even Elijah, according to Rabbinic legend, received a rebuke when he exclaimed, "I have been very jealous for the Lord God of Hosts." And it was intimated to him from heaven that there is just a possibility that it is his own person for which he shows so much zeal. This is indeed the great danger of every mission of this nature, that man is very often liable to confuse his own cause with that of God. I remember to have read somewhere a conversation between two American statesmen. In the heat of the argument the one quoted the well-known dictum of Johnson, "Patriotism is the last refuge of a scoundrel." Whereupon, the other retorted, "Sir, you overlook the possibilities of reform and progress." The history of Reconstruction unfortunately showed that the retort was not without a grain of truth.

Even more characteristic is Lincoln's answer given to a delegation of ministers from Chicago, urging him to issue a Proclamation of Emancipation before he considered it fit to do so. One of the ministers felt it his duty to make a more searching appeal to the President's conscience. Just as they were retiring, he turned and said to Lincoln: "What you have said to us, Mr. President, compels me to say to you in reply that it is a message to you from our Divine Master, through me, commanding you, sir, to open the doors of bondage, that the slave may go free!" Generally, "the master of men" followed the counsel of old sages, listening politely to every advice offered to him and deciding as seemed to him best:

> Listen to every counsel,
> And the best of them choose,
> And make the counsel of thy heart to stand;
> For there is none more faithful unto thee than it.

But he had little patience with dogmatism of the kind just cited, and his answer was: "That may be, sir, for I have studied this question by night and by day, for weeks and for months, but if it is, as you say, a message from your Divine Master, is it not odd that the only channel He could send it by was that roundabout route by way of that awful wicked city of Chicago?" This is the version given by Schuyler Colfax in his "Reminiscences" of Lincoln, but there is also another version of it, in which the uncharitable remark about the metropolis of the West is omitted. It reads: "I hope it will not be irreverent for me to say that if it is probable that God would reveal His will to others on a point so connected with my duty, it might be supposed He would reveal it directly to me. . . . Whatever shall appear to be God's will, I will do." The fact is Lincoln recognized no other medium for this divine revelation than "the will of the people, constitutionally expressed, which is the ultimate law for all." This is indeed the "mystery of democracy, or sentiment of the equality before God of all His creatures," which assumes that all the world's people are prophets, but at the same time perceives in the Constitution of the United States the best guarantee against false prophets.

As far as Lincoln himself is concerned, all the false prophets have disappeared, for indeed there were false prophets both among the Republicans and the Democrats who predicted most dire consequences from Lincoln's election. In a letter to General J. M. Schofield, who had to contend so much with the various factions within the Republican Party itself, Lincoln wrote, "If both factions, or neither, shall abuse you, you will probably be about right. Beware of being assailed by one and praised by the other." Lincoln passed through both stages, having been first assailed by all parties, and now praised by all, even by many eminent Southerners who do not fail to recognize his greatness. And thus he is doubly right.

The half century that has wellnigh elapsed since his death has dispelled the mists that encompassed him on earth. Men now not only recognize the right which he championed, but behold in him the standard of righteousness, of liberty, of conciliation and truth. In him, as it were personified, stands the Union, all that is best and noblest and enduring in its principles, in which he devoutly believed and strove mightily to save. When today, the world celebrates the century of his existence, he has become the ideal of both North and South, of a common country, composed not only of the factions that once confronted each other in war's dreadful array, but of the myriad thousands

that have since found in the American nation the
hope of the future and the refuge from age-entrenched
wrong and absolution.   To them Lincoln, his life,
his history, his character, his entire personality,
with all its wondrous charm and grace, its sobriety.
patience, self-abnegation and sweetness, has come to
be the very prototype of a rising humanity.

A certain Jewish saint who had the misfortune to
survive the death of his greatest disciple, is recorded
to have exclaimed: "O Lord, thou shouldst be grateful to me that I have trained for Thee so noble a soul."
This is somewhat too bold, but we may be grateful
to God for having given us such a great soul as Lincoln, "who, under God, gave this nation a new birth
of freedom," and to our dear country, which by its
institutions and its people rendered possible the greatness for which Abraham Lincoln shall stand forever.

BENNO BADT.*

THE death of Professor Doctor Benno Badt, which occurred on the 16th of April, 1909, will be felt as an irreparable loss by the Breslau community, and not less by his numerous friends on both sides of the Atlantic.

Doctor Badt was born in the year 1844 at Schwersenk, in the Grand-Duchy of Posen, but he emigrated at a very early age to Breslau, the capital of Prussian Silesia. There he took up a double course of studies, secular and theological; the former at the gymnasium and university, the latter at the Jewish Theological Seminary of that city. From both these institutions he graduated with distinction. The guiding spirit of the Breslau Seminary at that period was its famous director, R. Zecharias Frankel, assisted by such men of renown as Graetz, Bernays and Joel. Badt, however, never made use of his Rabbinic diploma, his preference having been for the scholastic career. He thus entered the Johannes Gymnasium as instructor, where in due course of time he was promoted to the rank of Oberlehrer, and then to that of Professor, which office he held to the end of his life. The subjects on which he lectured were the classical languages, Greek and Latin. He was also a fine English scholar, and, if I am not mistaken, he gave instruction in that language for some time.

But though he refused to make a profession of

*Paper contributed to the *American Hebrew*, May 7, 1909.

the Rabbinate, he remained a Rabbi all his life in
the best sense of this term. When the authorities
of the Seminary remonstrated with him for declining
to accept a call from a congregation, he is reputed to
have answered that he chose to remain a "Welt-
priester" (lay brother), in which capacity he might
accomplish more good. And so he did. Though
moving largely, by reason of his profession, in a pagan
world, he reserved in it a small corner sacred to his
favorite subject, closely bordering on Jewish literature. I refer to his Hellenistic studies, in which Jew
and pagan meet so closely, and in which he was considered a specialist. The results of these studies
were given to the world in his various treatises on
the Sybilline Oracles. Only a few months ago he
published an excellent translation of Philo's *Vita
Mosis*, equipped with a scientific apparatus of the
highest order. But this was only a small fraction
of what he could do and might have done, had his
professional duties not been of so absorbing a nature.
Both in his conversation and in his correspondence he
would dwell with intense expectancy on the time when
circumstances would enable him to retire from his
post in the Gymnasium in order to devote himself
entirely to the study of his favorite subject.

He was also greatly interested in the problem of
religious education, to the solution of which he contributed both by direct teaching in religious schools
and by many an essay in various pedagogic periodicals and societies. His "Kinderbibel" for use at
home and in school is, as I understand, one of the

most popular books of this kind in Germany. As to his *Richtung* (religious views), he remained, in spite of all his devotion to Hellenistic literature, a staunch conservative Jew all his life. Or perhaps it was because of this devotion that he was a Conservative Jew, as was the case with many a Jewish savant that made a specialty of the Septuagint, Philo and the cognate productions of Alexandrian Judaism. Hellenism is certainly one of the most important phenomena in our history, but if it teaches anything in the way of a practical lesson, it is that any attempt to dispense with the sacred language and to emphasize the universal elements at the expense of the ceremonial law and its national aspect, must result in disaster. The center of gravity of Judaism must remain in Judaism, and may never be placed outside of it.

Besides his scholarly pursuits, he was also one of the most active men in the Breslau Jewish community. He served on the Board of Jewish Representatives of that city, where he always both urged and enforced the claims of the conservative section of the community. Charity was a specialty of his: he was very liberal in his contributions to every worthy cause, and, what was more, he made others imitate his example, for which his position as committeeman on various philanthropic societies of Breslau gave him ample opportunity. Struggling students repaired to him freely, and were sure of being received hospitably. He was always ready to accord them advice and even material support. For all sorts of men of intelligence, taste and culture his house was a favorite

rendezvous, and they accounted it a privilege and a
delight to spend an evening in his company and the
company of his accomplished wife.

But better than all his activities was Badt himself. To know Badt was to love and to honor him.
This was the case both with Jew and Christian,
liberal or conservative. He was held in high esteem
by the whole community, and deeply revered by his
colleagues and pupils. Indeed, his love of truth
was proverbial in Breslau. I am convinced, and so
I am sure are all who knew him, that he would rather
have suffered martyrdom than speak or even think
an untruth. For he was, indeed, "a man who feared
God as well in private as in public, acknowledged
the truth and spake truth in his heart."

The story is told of a Rabbi, who paid a visit to
a friend on his sickbed, that he suddenly broke out
in tears. "I cry," he said, "over that beauty, that it
should rot in the dust." A more beautiful soul than
Badt, more noble, more upright, more Jewish, has
rarely been among us, and this soul beautified and
ennobled and hallowed many another soul with
which it came in closer contact. And they all will
join in the cry coming from Breslau, and mingle their
tears with those shed by his friends and pupils. They
will bless the hour that brought them in touch with
Badt, and will cherish his memory until they themselves become a memory.

הה לי ידידי מפרידת אח
שמו רשפיה בלפי אח
פרוד ימיתני בכל יום עד
בכו למותי . . . . . .

THE BEGINNINGS OF JEWISH
"WISSENCHAFT."*

SEVERAL years ago, when Death began to reap his harvest among the ancient masters of Jewish learning, I happened to attend a gathering of students, all of whom acknowledged themselves as the disciples of Zunz, Graetz, Geiger, Frankel, and their colleagues. They had assembled with the purpose of holding a sort of informal memorial service, in memory of these great men. I say "informal," because, instead of commencing with eloquent addresses, enlarging on the merits of the departed, the meeting opened with a long silence. I must further state that these students belonged to a school which held the most peculiar views. For instance, Wellhausen was not considered by them as the oracle in problems bearing upon the rise and development of Jewish sects, nor were for them the views of Schuerer and Bousset decisive in questions relating to Rabbinism. They had even their doubts as to the infallibility of Protestant encyclopedias in matters bearing upon Jewish history and Jewish theology; they were old-fashioned enough to prefer consulting, in all these matters, such authorities as were able to derive their information from the Hebrew sources in the original

---

*Lecture forming the first of a series of ten Lectures on the Genizah, delivered at the Dropsie College, Philadelphia, 1910. It appears here in expanded form.

and did actually read them before passing judgment upon their importance or worthlessness. They were thus, in their researches, mainly dependent upon those whose disappearance left them, to use the old Talmudic expression, an "orphaned generation." The mourning was sincere and too deep for words, and the assembly abandoned itself to contemplation, or rather to brooding over its great losses.

The silence, however, was soon broken by a remark coming from the Nestor of the gathering, running as follows: "True, my friends, the loss of these masters is irreparable, but, forget not that their work was completely done, to which they could not have added even if a longer life had been granted to. them. Life was not any more worth living for them. Our libraries have already been explored; our manuscripts have already been examined; our catalogues have already been compiled; our history has already been written; our liturgy has already been described, and the greatest part of the Talmud and the Midrashim have already been scientifically edited. The records of the past are now a matter of the past. The future affords little scope for learned research." These words were meant as a tribute to the dead, and not less as a consolation to the living. But the speaker proved to be rather a Job's comforter, implying, as his words did, that those of the younger generation had better abdicate their scholarly activity, and wait patiently for absorption into the great "intellectual All"—or, perhaps, betake themselves into the region of "Latter-day Seers and Prophets."

A heated discussion then ensued, some siding with the speaker, others contesting the truth of his sweeping statement.

The arguments of the speaker were largely of a statistical nature. He pointed proudly at the stately arrays of shelves, accommodating a large number of volumes, which, for want of some better term, may be roughly comprised under the designation of Judaica, and certainly imposing by their quantity; as to quality, suffice it to mention that they included such works as Zunz's *Gottesdienstlichen Vortraege*, Fraenkel's *Introductions to the Mishna and the Talmud of Jerusalem*, Geiger's *Urschrift*, Graetz's *History*, and Steinschneider's *Catalogue of the Bodleian Library*. If we further add the great number of dissertations on Jewish topics, and the larger number of articles scattered over various periodicals, which together embrace almost all departments of Jewish *Wissenschaft*, we shall recognize at once the force of the argument of our pessimistic speaker. Yet, he was entirely wrong in his conclusions. Like all statisticians, he was too much impressed by numbers, and, as a pessimist, he had no eye for the future with its glorious possibilities.

The growth of Jewish *Wissenschaft* is a matter of comparatively recent date, going back only a few generations. This does not imply that Jewish *Wissenschaft* is, as some claim, a product of the Reform or Rationalistic movement in Judaism. Rationalism, as history testifies, has never proved a real friend to learning. It has little desire for the opinions of the ancients; and it is amply satisfied with its five- or eight-cubit library, in which there is hardly room for the Bible, and certainly none for the vast literature which the Bible has produced. In its initial stages, while public opinion was still anxious for precedent and authority, it may sometimes have enlisted *Wissenschaft* as its auxiliary; but it emancipated itself from it soon enough, as from a useless burden, when the people became callous and indifferent and put their Judaism into the hands of a receiver. It may further be pointed out that the masters of Jewish learning were not slow to see that the Rationalistic or Reform movement was not always a very trustworthy ally. Any one who doubts this might pause to ask himself how it came to pass that such men as Krochmal, Rappaport, Zunz, Frankel, Sachs, Jacob Bernays, Luzzatto, Chayess, Joel, Graetz, Steinschneider and a host of others, were either directly hostile to this movement, or abandoned it after a short connection, or at least remained entirely indifferent to its claims. If a census should be taken of all those who made their mark in any department of Jewish learning by a really original contribution— I am not speaking of dilettanti and journalists—it would be found that at least 90 per cent. were either directly opposed to the Reform movement, or ignored its existence altogether. Did Jewish students as early as the middle of the last century foresee, perhaps, that "modernity," notwithstanding its "enthusiasm about the study of the sources," would in the end prove a menace to learning, which it really

is in our days, parading its contempt of all scholarship, just as the Chasidim did at an early period of
their existence?

As a fact, the study of the sources did not yield
the results which the Reform movement had expected.
Philology may have detected many a flaw in many a
Talmudic argument, and proved that the interpretations of the more ancient sources of the Babylonian
or even the Palestinian schools were homiletical
rather than exegetical; whilst history may have discovered that certain usages and even certain beliefs
were of a foreign origin; but the same instruments
of research helped to reveal the following important
facts.   First, that Judaism was an organism with a
natural growth, rooted in the Torah; the inheritance
of the congregation of Jacob, not the artificial product of Rabbinical conferences, commissions and
sub-committees.   It grew out of the tree of Life,
the Torah, whose commandments were never put
to a vote; never did Jewish authorities meet with the
purpose of accepting a foreign belief or un-Jewish
usages.   The injunction of the Law—"Inquire not
after their gods, saying 'How did these nations serve
their gods?   Even so I will do likewise' " (Deut.
12: 30)—an injunction specially applicable to
worship, was always before their eyes.   That certain
foreign beliefs and foreign usages should creep in
was unavoidable, as Israel neither could nor would
shut itself off entirely from the influences of the outside
world.   But they had to pass through that process
of assimilation to things Jewish, and of elimination

of things un-Jewish, which was strongly at work
in the Synagogue; and through this their trans-
formation and complete conversion to Judaism, so
to speak, were effected. It will suffice to recall here—
with particular reference to beliefs—the history of
the "Logos" in its various metamorphoses in the
Church, and its different history in the Synagogue.

Secondly, research has proved that the Torah,
even within the limits of the Pentateuch, is the very
life of Judaism, and that its abrogation means death.
Against this stronghold, which, as history testifies,
Israel defended with its very life, were directed all
the attacks of both Pagan and Christian fanaticism,
and the battle is now continued by our modern "amateur Gentiles." The Sabbath and the Covenant of
Abraham are especially mentioned as the commandments of the Torah for which Israel had undergone martyrdom. And the mere thought that the
abolition of such laws should be discussed and reported
upon by appointed commissions is appalling and
abhorrent to the Jewish historical conscience. The
same can be said of the retention of Hebrew in the
Synagogue; for though a certain Halachah offers
concessions in this respect, history teaches that
Judaism, by the mere instinct of self-preservation,
rarely, if ever, made use in the Synagogue of any other
but the sacred language. The assertion that the
Jewish historian Herzfeld, in his objection to the
replacing of Hebrew by German in the Synagogue
was moved by sentiment or romantic reasons, cannot
be entertained for a moment. Any man who has ever
read Herzfeld's *Geschichte des Volkes Israel*—which is,
indeed, very hard reading, and taxes all the powers

of the student—knows how little its author was given to romanticism and sentimentalism. A more sober and dry—though a very painstaking—scholar never lived. But he was an historian after all, and could not well agree to the entire banishment of the Hebrew language from the Synagogue; for this would mean, as he himself expresses it, "The abandoning of our positive historical standpoint." Altogether it seems that these "hard-shell" modernists think that they have only to stigmatize a man as a romanticist, or a thing as savouring of romanticism, to eliminate them from further consideration. The savage chief in Africa thinks the Christian missionary, who endeavors to beautify his cottage by his little garden of flowers, a useless romanticist, as he could better employ his time and his money by cultivating sweet potatoes and corn. The Lyceum philosopher, with his universal ignorance, looks contemptuously upon the quiet scholar who is blinding himself with the deciphering of MSS. or the interpretation of the great ideas of the heroes of the world, as a romanticist, who could better spend his time in the writing of a slashing article or an eloquent address, which, indeed, would be more profitable to his reputation with the mob. George Eliot describes romanticism as the thing which helps to fill some dull blanks with love and knowledge. The mission of the scholar in our time seems to be to fill some dull minds with love and knowledge of things sacred and sublime, which things *bourgeois* philosophy declares to be and endeavors to make blank and void.

Thirdly, research has taught that universalistic Judaism, propagated by means of abolishing the Law

and at the risk of the final absorption of Israel by its
surroundings, is in contradiction to the teachings of
the Bible, the teachings of the Talmud, and all
Jewish opinion that has come down to us from antiquity, from the Middle Ages, and even from modern
times as late as the middle of the last century.   It
is anti-prophetical—unless, in a Christian spirit, we
sterilize the nationalistic passages pervading the whole
of the Bible.   It is anti-Rabbinical—unless we tear
out passages from the contexts and pervert their
meaning.   In brief, it is non-Jewish and un-Jewish.
It has no root and no room in Jewish thought, and
derives its pedigree from Paul's Epistles.

It is not, then, to reform tendencies that we are
to look for the main impulse and continuous encour-
agement of Jewish learning.   The scientific movement
began long before the looming of Rationalism.   The
first attempt, indeed, towards the building up of a
Jewish science was given by R. Azariah de Rossi,
the author of the *Meor Enayim,* who flourished about
the end of the sixteenth century.   De Rossi, however,
was out of date with his criticism, and for reasons
which cannot be entered upon here he left no real
impress on his time.   More successful in their attempts, though they were hardly conscious of the
nature of their work of regeneration, were two
Lithuanian Jews of the second half of the eighteenth
century, R. Elijah, of Wilna, commonly called "the
Gaon of Wilna," and R. Jechiel Heilperin, of Minsk.
The latter is best known by his work, *Seder Ha-
Doroth,* or the *Chronology of the Generations,* which
deals especially with the successive generations of

the Tannaim and Amoraim. It is now superseded, in parts at least, by works of a more recent date, but only one who knows for how many centuries this branch of study was almost entirely neglected, can appreciate what it meant to prove for the first time that there existed such a thing as a science of Rabbinical succession, which alone can establish the claims of tradition. The book further proves the danger of the terrible thing called anachronism, against which scholars have always to be on their guard. We have now some better books on this subject, but they would never have been written without the aid of the monumental work of Heilperin, who first collected the materials in a systematic way and so made possible the task of the historians, who both exploited and patronized him.

Of even greater significance was the work of "the Gaon." If there ever was a prince in Israel, reigning supreme in its intellectual world, it was the Gaon of Wilna. He mastered it all; the whole of the Scriptures, as well as its Targumim; the whole of the Mishnah, as well as the Tosephta and other products of the Tannaim; the whole of the Talmud; the Talmud of Babylon, as well as the Talmud of Jerusalem; the whole of the Midrashim; the Midrash Halacha, as well as the Midrash Haggada, in addition to that vast Responsa literature of Commentaries, Codes, Responsa, philosophic and mystical treatises, and edifying works, which grew up during the last eighteen centuries. What is of pre-eminent importance is his attitude towards the commentaries; more particularly the commentaries to the earlier Rabbinic

works which embody Jewish tradition, such as the
Talmud, the Mishnah, and the Midrash, etc. The
defect of many of these commentaries consisted
largely in the fact that they failed to comply with
the principle laid down by R. Hai Gaon. This is
to the effect that the first duty of a commentator is
to convey correctly the views of his author, and not
to intrude upon them with views of his own. The
rationalistic, and not less the mystical schools were,
as is well known, great sinners in this respect. However, it is not for modernism to throw the first stone.
In our eagerness to adapt Judaism to all things possible and impossible, we occasionally force upon the
Talmud and the Bible up-to-date opinions, upon
which Sage and Seer could have looked only with
horror and dismay. But even those commentators
who owed no allegiance to any particular school,
have not always been successful in their endeavor
to give us the exact meanings of the words of their
authors. And this for the simple reason that these
words often came down to them in such a fragmentary
form or such a corrupt text, that they defied all
explanation. This is the case with all ancient literature, as everybody knows who has read a classic
coming from antiquity. But the difficulties increase
with the Talmud, when one considers its peculiar
form, its elliptical sentences, its rambling style, and,
above all, the abrupt and uncertain methods of
its compilers.

These difficulties the Gaon endeavored to sur-
mount by applying to the Rabbinic literature the
old Rabbinic rule, "The words of the Torah are poor

in the one place, but wealthy in another!" Through
his acquaintance with the *whole* of the Torah, he had
no difficulty in discovering the wealthy places. If
there was a difficult passage in this or that tractate,
he showed, by giving a reference to some other place,
that it was wanting in some words or lines. Obscure
passages in the Mishnah he tried to eludicate by
parallel passages in the Tosephta, or in the Mechilta
or the Sifra. The complicated controversies of the
Babylonian Talmud he tried to explain by comparing
them with the passages in the simpler Talmud of
Jerusalem. If we remember that it was just these
ancient Rabbinic productions, which were neglected
for centuries, we shall at once appreciate his greatness. He almost re-discovered them. Nor was he
satisfied with the mere joy of the discovery; he wrote
commentaries or glosses in a brief, concise way to
almost the whole of the ancient Jewish literature,
including the Talmud of Babylon, always remaining
true to his principle that the author has to explain
himself. With this great contribution the foundations for textual criticism were laid.

The other places, however, in which the wealth of
the Torah is to be found have, in numberless cases,
proved to be manuscripts or rare prints. Unfortunately, they were largely out of the reach of the Gaon.
A few manuscripts may, perhaps, have been in his
possession, as is implied occasionally by some of his
emendations. But, even if this be the case, their
number must have been very small; it may be fairly
doubted whether the Gaon had seen in his life more
than half a dozen. As to rare prints and early

editions, I hardly believe that he ever had the opportunity to make use of them; the regular Hebrew
library, in a Russian community consisted as a rule
of cheap editions of the Bible, the Talmud, and other
standard books of the Rabbinic literature essential to
the practicing rabbi, but little beyond this. Private
collections were very few. As to public collections,
neither the Polish, nor the Russian, nor even the
German Government possessed at that time many
Hebrew books in their national libraries; whilst the
few libraries in France and in Italy and other places,
which included Hebrew collections, were not accessible to the Jews. As far as our knowledge goes (but
I must admit that the matter has never been properly
investigated), the first Jew who was admitted to any
public library was R. Chayim Joseph David Azulai.
He made an entry of this fact in his diary, *Maagal
Tob*. The great event occurred on the 6th of "Te-
beth," in the year 1778, when he went with his
friend, a Gentile, to the library of Paris, in which he
saw thousands of manuscripts "in all wisdoms" (or
.subjects). He saw also hundreds of Hebrew manuscripts, a Bible on parchment, 717 years old, and ever
so many books on philosophy, astronomy, early
Kabbala and other important books. This liberality
towards Azulai was probably a consequence of his
having enjoyed the reputation that it was in his power
to work miracles by means of amulets. The French
nobles of the period preceding the great Revolution,
with all their rationalism, were by no means insensible
to these occult powers of Azulai, and asked both for
his blessing and his amulets. But it must be admitted

that Azulai made the best of his opportunities, as will be seen from another entry in the same diary: "Thursday:—The Marquis and his wife came and seated themselves near me, and she asked me to pray for her. She also told me that she reads the Bible. Further, that she sometimes sees angels and demons, who address her. Among others she also mentioned the Baal-Shem of London[this the well-known Falk]. She told me also that a Jew gave her a Kabbalistic book and recounted to me other wonderful things. I answered several questions which she put to me. And on that day I went to the Library of Manuscripts and copied a part of the commentaries of R. Isaiah of Trani. I went about the Library, in which they have ever so many manuscripts written in numerous languages, and bearing upon all wisdoms and religions. The collection also contains a long book written on broad leaves of the palm branch— Lulab," (perhaps he meant papyrus).

To return to the Gaon. That Rabbi Elijah of Wilna was not quite insensible to the wealth of the Torah buried in inaccessible MSS. may be concluded from the book, (*Rab Poolim*) by his son, R. Abraham Wilna. R. Abraham died in 1809, but his book remained in manuscript for eighty-five years, when it was published by Herr Chanes. Its contents often remind us of Zunz's *Gottesdienstlichen Vortraege*, but it was chiefly intended to furnish a list of the lost Midrashim and other ancient Rabbinic works known only from quotations, and it was written with the set purpose of inaugurating a systematic search after these works. "How shall we search," R. Abraham says, "if we are quite ignorant of our losses?" Here the influence of the Gaon is visible; for the regular Rabbinic students of the time were, as already indicated, quite satisfied with the literature at their disposal, which was adequate for practical purposes. Besides R. Abraham, we may mention here a few other Russian scholars who came under the Gaon's influence; such as R. Abigdor of Slonim, the commentator of the Tosephta; and R. Enoch Zindel, the annotator of several Midrashim. The greatest, though the youngest, of this school was, undoubtedly, R. Raphael Rabbinowitz, the author of the *Variae Lectiones* to the Talmud of Babylon, which is a marvel of industry, learning, and sound criticism. Unfortunately, the work was interrupted by the death of the author when it reached the fifteenth volume. How far R. Isaiah Pick of Breslau, who worked on the same lines as the Gaon, was influenced by him, I am unable to say.

But neither Pick nor the Gaon had any immediate influence upon their successors in Germany. The rationalistic school, succeeding Mendelssohn, had very little use for manuscripts. I dare say that even the printed books were too many for them. They were a set of mere dilettanti who cared to study as little and write as much as possible. One need only read Peter Beer's book on *The Sects* and Hertz Homberg's *Catechism* to see how little the one was of an historian and the other of a theologian.

Jewish science in Germany only began with the ebb of the rationalistic wave, which swept over Germany during the French Revolution. When it

has spent its force, men go back to history, and the
past is restored to its rights but not to its wrongs.
This tendency was felt everywhere, by Krochmal,
Rappaport, and Chayess in the East, as well as Zunz,
Fraenkel, Sachs, Graetz, and others in the West.
To mention here only the first of these luminaries
in each series, we can point to Rappaport's famous
biographies of R. Saadya Gaon, of R. Nathan, the
author of the *Aruch*, of R. Hai Gaon, the last of the
Gaonim, of R. Eliezer Kalir, the great liturgical
poet, and of R. Hananel, and of R. Nissim of Cairo-
wan.   In Germany we have Zunz's *Gottesdienstlichen
Vortraege*.   Each of these productions was epoch-
making in its time, opening new worlds to students.
The men, for instance, who formed the subject of
Rappaport's researches were not mere individuals,
but heads of schools, of either Talmudical or liturgical schools, as in the case of Nathan and Kalir;
Hananel and Nissim, again, ushered in a new wpoch
in which the Torah was decentralised from Babylon,
and new seats of learning were established in different
parts of the world.   As to Zunz's *Gottesdienstlichen
Vortraege*, it is enough to say that it is practically a
history of tradition in its Agadic aspect.   As is clear
from the contents of the book, it very soon outgrew
the narrow plan of the author, who began it with the
purpose of showing the propriety of the sermon in
the vernacular in the Synagogue.   An essay of twenty
pages would have amply served this purpose.   Nor
was there, as subsequent history showed, any real
objection to the sermon as such.   No protest was ever
raised in Russia or Poland or Lithuania against the

Maggid or the Darshan. The real objection was, in many cases, to the undue importance given to the sermon, which made it likely to supersede worship, "so that it was he, not He, who was the center of attraction," and to the preacher himself, who was not in every congregation distinguished by his loyalty to traditional Judaism, and lastly, to the contents of the sermon, which were not always in harmony with the teachings of Judaism.

The books which Zunz and Rappaport and their contemporaries consulted in their gigantic works were certainly more numerous than those which were at the disposal of the Gaon. The later masters had also the advantage of being acquainted more or less with the classical idioms, as well as the cognate Semitic dialects, which, with the exception of the Aramaic, remained a sealed book to the Gaon and his school. But the number of manuscripts they consulted was certainly not large. It is enough to record here that Zunz had hardly occasion to consult half a dozen when writing the *Gottesdienstlichen Vortraege*. It was only in later life that he examined the collections of the Bodleian Library in Oxford and of the British Museum in London, which laid the foundation for his works on the liturgy and hymnology of the Synagogue. He travelled also in Italy, where he examined the contents of various libraries, but, as is clear from this article, *Die Hebraeischen Handschriften in Italien*, he was not admitted to the Vatican. There, as he expresses himself in a rather midrashic manner, "the Dragon was still blocking the way to the Hebrew collections." Much smaller were the

opportunities for using manuscripts given to Rappaport, Chayess, Krochmal, and other builders of
Jewish science. Rappaport's main source for information contained in manuscripts was the great Samuel
David Luzzatto of Padua, who supplied his friend
as well as other scholars with extracts from his library,
which was a real treasure of rare prints and Hebrew
manuscripts. The majority of workers, however,
had little or no access to great libraries, and were
dependent upon the small collections of their native
cities, which both in Germany and the bordering
countries, as a rule, were neither rich nor very select.
Considering, on the one hand, the vast domain of
Rabbinic literature extending over two thousand
years, and on the other, the poverty of Jewish scholars
and the paucity of those able to travel extensively,
it is clear that it was only a very small proportion of
their work to which they could apply the critical
apparatus which largely depends on great libraries.
It will suffice to state here the fact that neither Weiss,
the author of the *History of Tradition*, nor Friedmann, the greatest of our editors of ancient Rabbinical texts, was ever in a position to travel for the
purpose of examining the contents of the great libraries of Europe. The only collections to which they
had access were the Vienna Beth-Hamidrash Library,
and the few Hebrew MSS. deposited in the Imperial
Library of Austria.

Now we are thoroughly grateful for the good
things received, but there is still much more in store
for us to be received. The *Gottesdienstlichen Vortraege*, which will always remain a standard work,

is now, in many places, in need of revision, because of the various Rabbinic works published from manuscript since 1835. The editions of Friedmann, which are and will always remain models of scientific workmanship, would also bear a new edition, especially the Mechilta and the Sifre, for which he hardly had any manuscript at his disposal. In the Midrash Agada, Buber was especially active, and we are grateful to him for ever so many smaller and larger Agadic works, which he published from manuscripts; but of the main Midrashim, that is, the Midrash Rabba to the Five Books of Moses, we have only about a third part of the Midrash to Genesis properly edited by Dr. Theodor. Of the Tosephta, we have an edition of Zuckermandl, which, however imperfect, gives us the Erfurt and Vienna manuscripts of this Tannaitic collection. On the other hand, we have as yet no scientific edition of the Misnah, the main authority of traditional Judaism. All that we possess is a reprint of the Cambridge manuscript, and a good edition of *Pirke Aboth*, by the late Dr. Taylor. But of the most important manuscript, which is in Parma, and of another in the possession of the Budapest Academy, hardly any use has been made. Of the Talmud of Babylon, we have the *Variae Lectiones* compiled by Rabbinowitz, but his work, as mentioned above, remains unfinished because of his early death. For a proper edition of the Talmud of Jerusalem, we are only now beginning to collect materials.

It is evident, from the preceding remarks, that our libraries have not yet been thoroughly explored. Indeed, they would bear exploration for another generation; and even such as are most accessible, the British Museum and the Bodleian Library, are by no means exhausted. As to those less accessible, such as the Library at Parma, for instance, it is just touched on the surface, notwithstanding the many pilgrimages of Zunz, Berliner, and others. Nor have our great standard works been edited; we are just beginning to collect materials for really scientific editions. Our history, it is true, was written by Graetz, not to mention the contributions by Jost, Kayserling, and others. But the materials at their command were decidedly not of such a nature as to make the work of their successors superfluous. Let me not be misunderstood; I do not belong to the detractors of Graetz, whose history will always remain a monumental work. His notes and appendices are sufficient to place him in the foremost rank of our historians. It is true that he was not entirely impartial, but I have often observed that impartiality in history means as much as unsectarianism in religion. In religion, or rather theology, it implies admiring all other religions but your own; in history it stands for toadying to your antagonists and losing all understanding for yourself. It may further be true that a certain rationalism, from which few German scholars of that generation could emancipate themselves, made Graetz rather unfair towards mysticism and Russian Judaism; but this could easily be corrected. What his work really suffered in was the insufficiency of materials at his disposal. He had very few manuscripts to furnish him with facts, and thus was too much dependent on hypothesis. It will suffice to

mention here his chapter on the history of the Kar-
aites, which he wrote when hardly half a dozen lines
coming from Anan, the founder of the sect, were
known. Of these few lines, Graetz certainly made the
best use possible; but now we have large fragments
of Anan's *Book of Commandments*. Again, in his
account of the decentralization of the schools from
Babylon, Graetz had to spin history from a mere
legend. The facts simply did not exist. Sometimes
he had to rely on very faulty texts which he had no
means of controlling, because of his inability to travel
and to search after MSS. It is mortifying to think
that he never, for instance, had the opportunity to
read the Achimaaz Chronicle, which was buried in
some Spanish cloister and was edited only after his
death. How different would have been his presentation of the early history of the Jews in the South of
Italy and other places in the vicinity of the Medi-
terranean, had he had the good fortune to study this
most interesting document.

Foremost of all, it is to be noted that neither to
Graetz nor to the great majority of his contemporaries
was it granted to make sufficient use of the opening
of the Orient with its wealth of Hebrew manuscripts. Many were already gone when this event
took place. Even Rabbinowitz, who used a larger
number of manuscripts for his *Variae Lectiones* than
any other Jewish author has utilized for the edition
of a single work, was in the possession of hardly more
than one Oriental manuscript, which was presented
to him by the Rabbi of Cairo. It was only late in
the sixties of the last century that communication

was established with the Orient through the efforts of the famous traveler, Jacob Saphir of Jerusalem. His travels to Yemen placed us in the possession of quite a new class or family of MSS., till then entirely unknown. It gave us new grammarians, new commentators to the Bible, new liturgies, new Divans, both sacred and secular, and new Midrashim. But, unfortunately, in 1870, when the first results of his newly found treasures were published, many of our great scholars were already gone, whilst the few who remained were almost all too old for work. Zunz himself, as far as I know, only had occasion to describe one or two Yemen manuscripts of a liturgical nature. Saphir was followed by other travellers; particularly by the notorious Shapiro, who furnished the European libraries and museums with many a forgery, but also with many a genuine old manuscript coming from Yemen. Amongst these latter, the most important was probably the Midrash Haggadol, which, in itself, forms a large library. It is a sort of homiletical commentary to the Pentateuch in five volumes; but it restored to us many extracts from Tannaitic works, whose existence was only faintly guessed by scholars. The greatest gift, however, which the Orient has given to us is the Cairo Genizah, which, with the abundance of its material, the variety of its contents, and the wealth of its historical documents, has made us all feel that the light has come again from the East, illumining our past and strengthening our hope for the future, as no other event in the scholarly world during the last centuries had done. Verily the life of the student is once more worth living.

THE TEST THE RABBI SHOULD APPLY.*

PRECIOUS is the seventh," is an old Jewish
adage, and it is particularly precious to me in
view of the fact that it is for the seventh time that
we are gathered in this hall to confer the degrees of
Rabbi and Doctor upon our students. It is a sort
of Sabbatical year in the existence of the reorganized
Seminary, inviting in a certain measure to rest and
recreation, but even more to thought and reflection.

The subject nearest to our thoughts on this
solemn occasion is, as hardly need be said, the office
of the Rabbi, his position in the community, and his
significance for the perpetuation of Judaism. I
often had occasion to speak of all these matters both
at the Commencements and at other public gatherings, so that it is almost impossible to avoid repetition. However, the nearness of the Feast of the
Revelation, for which we are all now preparing (or
ought to prepare), suggests some thoughts which,
if not quite new, will certainly be timely. I am thinking of the interpretation given by the Rabbis to the
commandment, "Thou shalt not take the name of
the Lord, thy God in vain." This commandment
some Rabbis explain to mean, "Accept no dignity of
which thou art not worthy." Another Rabbi further
illustrates it with the words, "I, God, am called the
Holy One, and thou art called holy. Behold, if thou

*Address delivered at the Graduating Exercises of the Seminary,
June 5, 1910.

dost not possess all the qualities of holiness, accept no dignity." The dignity of which our sages speak in this place is that of Judge and Rabbi in their capacity as leaders of the community; and the special divine attribute which they expect in the leader of a community is, as you see, holiness.

Holiness is a wide subject, offering many aspects, as indeed all abstract qualities do, but I will only urge here one or two of these which are in need of particular emphasis. One of its main aspects, according to our sages, is absolute self-denial. Indeed, they teach that he who accepts any public office with the purpose of deriving from it any personal gain commits an act of gross immorality. I do not think that our sages would have objected to the maintenance of the Rabbi by his congregation. The highest ideal, as I had once occasion to mention, was that the Rabbi should impart his spiritual bounties to his congregation in the manner divine in which all blessing is a mere act of grace. But except in very rare cases, conditions made this ideal unattainable, and it was soon found necessary that the grace should just as much be exercised on the part of the community providing for the material needs of the Rabbi, as on the part of the Rabbi, who is to watch over the spiritual needs of the community. It was, however, never thought that the call of this sacred office should exactly become a regular profession in the sense of a bread-winning occupation. The divine call which urged the young man to devote himself to the profession of the Rabbi always preccded the formal call of the community with its appointments and stipulated contract. Many famous men in Israel who wielded the greatest authority over their contemporaries, and even over posterity, remained throughout their lives without such a formal call. Maimonides, for instance, never received such a call, and yet he was considered the spiritual head of Egypt and the neighboring countries. And least of all would the greatness of the Rabbi ever have been measured by the favorable conditions regarding salary and other material advantages stipulated in such a formal call, which seems to have become the regular standard of Rabbinical authority in our times.

Humility and meekness and sweet submission are other features of self-denial. The holy man is certainly not a respecter of persons, nor does he bow to current opinion when not in harmony with his convictions. He is fearless and straightforward. Yet he is distinguished by a certain reticence, by a certain delicacy of feeling, which make him shrink from everything loud, sensational, and the intruding of his personality upon the public. He glories in his mission, but you will certainly never find him doing anything aiming at the glorifying of the missionary.

Even in his praise of his friends and his colleagues he is sparing, strong as his devotion may be to them, as such praise is seldom free from a subconscious expectation of return, with interest. Indeed, in the constitution of a Rabbinical Association (or Club), which counted among its members such men as

Azulai, Galante and Buton, we find in the by-laws
that no member should ever mention a word in praise
of his colleagues, or even of their leaders. On the
other hand, everyone of them was bound to admonish
his friend of his shortcomings, which the latter had
not only to accept without resentment, but with
love and gratitude. I wish these saints would have
left us the minutes of their club. The difference
between these and the accounts of our present
gatherings, religious and social, would certainly
have been worth a study.

But let me remind you at once of the further
dictum of our sages, לא עַם הָאָרֶץ חסיד, "no ignorant
man can be a saint." Speaking in the presence of
Rabbis, I hardly need say that by ignorance I do not
mean the absence of knowledge as a consequence of
a deficient training, though, unfortunately, such
cases occur. However, these cases as a rule are more
in the class of "latter-day prophets" than of Rabbis.
What I mean by ignorance is that engendered by a
lack of will or opportunity to continue those studies,
the foundation of which was laid in halls such as
these. The consequence of this ignorance is deplor-
able: an utter thoughtlessness about all things
divine. The Rabbi is expected to "do things." Upon
this we are all agreed; but he should also have the
opportunity to think things. Young men in the
ministry sometimes come to me with the complaint
that the communities in which they are placed do
not offer a sufficient field of work. My answer in
certain cases is: "If you have time to spare from all

the manifold duties a congregation offers, social and
religious, the best thing you might do is to devote the
rest of your time to study." But I usually meet with
very little response, the feeling on the part of the
Rabbi being that the rumor of his being "addicted to
Jewish learning" will bring him into disrepute and
will only prove injurious to his career. Why this
should be so is a riddle to me. Europe, which many
have accepted as a model in so many respects, offers
us some of the best books of real scientific value
written by clergymen, Jewish as well as Christian.
Would it be indeed such a calamity if among the
hundreds of ministers we count in this country, we
would have at least a sprinkling of learned men, who
would, now and then, favor us with such pieces of
work as the *Jewish Eschatology from Daniel to Akiba*,
by Von Woltz, Stadt-Pfarrer, at Leonberg (Wuerthem-
berg), or *The Religious and Ethical Conceptions of
the Old Testament, the Apocrypha and the Pseudepigrapha*, by Ludwig Conrad, Pfarrer zu Klinkow bei
Prenzlau? Would it really bring disgrace upon
Israel in this country if its spiritual destinies would
now and then be presided over by men of the stamp
of Dr. Kohut and Dr. Jastrow, who left us the
greatest Rabbinical Dictionaries, or Herzfeld and
Sachs and Kayserling, who gave to the world the
best books on the most important periods of Jewish
history, or Dr. Szold, who bequeathed to us one of
the most lucid commentaries on the Book of Job?

We are fond of speaking of Judaism as a religion,
though we practically never define the nature of this

religion, our attitude towards its doctrines and precepts and promises, and the obligation it devolves
upon us.   But have you ever seen a great religion
without its learned ôrders or at least learned clergy?
And, least of all, how should Judaism, with its traditions of learning, with its vast literature, with the
prominent feature of Torah (teaching) subsist without
scholars, without students?   Maimonides tells us,
"And He (God) said unto us through Isaiah, the good
messenger of the nation, that the sign between Him
and us and the convincing pledge that Israel will
never perish is the fact that His Torah and His word
remain among us."   Do you believe that this pledge
still holds good when the Jewish laity is further from
any knowledge of the Torah, including the Bible,
than any other section of the community, whilst the
Jewish minister is expected to be anything and everything: an organizer, a social agitator, an expert in
all topics of the day, but is never expected to be a
sound Hebrew scholar?

It is true that we live here a more strenuous life
than they do in Europe, and that the demands on
the practical side are greater than they are elsewhere.
But what is life without thought, and, least of all,
what value has Jewish religious life without Jewish
religious thought?   Besides, I am only pleading for
a sprinkling or remnant which would be devoted to
this Jewish religious thought, but which may prove
a leaven to the community and a healthy and helpful
religious force to all their brethren in the pulpit.

I must further remark that when I speak here of
holiness I am thinking of Jewish holiness which, as

you will find in so many theological works, is always described as "the peculiar" Jewish conception of holiness. It just as much includes the ritual and ceremonial as the ethical holiness. Altogether, never forget that you are Jewish preachers, and that there is no other standard for you but that supplied by Judaism. Perhaps I may illustrate this counsel by the following story communicated by R. Solomon ibn Verga, in his *Shebet Jehudah*, which runs as follows: Among the exiles from Spain there was a Jew and his family, who, by reason of the epidemic which broke out in the boat which carried him away from his native country, was compelled to land on some desolate place remote from all human habitation. His wife, who was very delicate, became exhausted and died. Famished and worn out, he carried his two sick children, but at last fatigue and hunger overpowered him, and he fainted and fell down. When he awoke from his trance he found his two children dead by his side. He then rose to his feet and in his grief exclaimed: "Master of the world, much hast Thou done unto me which hastens my steps toward apostacy. But know it for a certainty that against the very will of those who dwell in heaven, a Jew I am and a Jew I shall remain, in spite of all the suffering Thou hast brought and may still bring over me."

My friends, we can well realize how this exile came to think that the power of heaven was against him. He was just fleeing from a country which was at that time perhaps the greatest world power history

had ever seen. Its Church was certainly the most
powerful one in the world, and certainly more universal than any Church ever was or ever will be.
Indeed, its missionaries were soon to overrun new
continents—the West Indies as well as the East
Indies, and if you have read, for instance, Parkman's
"History of Canada," you will admit that these missionaries were not entirely devoid of spirituality.
So, as it seemed to this poor exile, both the powers
on earth and the powers in heaven were arrayed
against Judaism. Thank God, we have now to fear
very little the powers on earth. The very country
which Spain was to discover and in which discovery
it reached the zenith of its power, was destined by
Providence to prove, in the course of history, the
refuge of the descendants of the very fellow-exiles
of this great Spanish Jew. And so in other parts of
the world, especially in Western Europe, Israel is
enjoying more or less the protection of the powers
on earth, giving them at least equality before the
law and guaranteeing in part the fruits of their
emancipation.

But it is, if I may say so, the imaginary powers
of heaven against which we have to be on our guard.
Ideals are put up, ignoring history and all its lessons
but appealing to theological commonplaces which
have a heavenly look about them. I know of no other
advice to give you but that you try all these new
ideals by the test of this Spanish Jew. Thus you will
hear a great deal about the ideal of a universal
religion. You will even be made to understand that

this was the ideal of our prophets, though by some accident or other they were misunderstood by the Jews for a period of eighteen hundred years or more. It is certainly very flattering to our pride and vanity to be told that it is in our power to become the spiritual conquerors of the world at the cost of a small sacrifice—of a small volume called the Pentateuch. But the only test you can apply to it is that of the poor Spanish exile. Will you after this conquest be Jews and remain Jews, or not? If it does not bear this test, you may be sure that the message is not a heavenly one. This test you can apply to all the points which are now the subject of controversy, such as the Sunday service, the gradual banishment of the Hebrew from the synagogue as the language of prayer and worship, and abolition of certain festivals in favor of more convenient days, the abrogation of almost the entire ritual law, the neglecting of every specific Jewish ceremony, the obliteration of all reference to Zion and Jerusalem from our liturgy, and many other points like these. You will be told that all this is done for the sake of heaven and for the great cause of religion. I need not enter into details, but I can only repeat what I have just said: Ask yourself seriously and honestly whether or not all this will bear the test of that Spanish Jew. "A Jew I am and a Jew I shall remain." If the latter be the case, then it is your sacred duty to prove yourself the descendants of the stiff-necked ones, and defy heaven as that Spanish exile did defy heaven and earth.

This Jewish standard may, to a certain extent, be also applied to the social work of the Rabbi. I am led to this remark by a passage which I have read in the book of an Englishman who recently traveled through this country. Among others, he also visited, as it seems, our charitable institutions and came a great deal into contact with settlement workers. This traveler reports that the head of a prominent settlement house made the remark to him that "the sentiment of pity and mercy as a motive of social service has become outworn." The new motive, he declares, is "a certain spirit of moral adventure, carrying a suggestion of statesmanship." Now, as Rabbis, you will probably take your share in social work which, as I hope, will become with everyone of you a part of his Rabbinical duties. I do not know what your attitude will be toward these moral adventures. I have some dread of all adventures, but I do not think myself competent to give an opinion about them. However, whatever your attitude may be, be Jews and remain Jews, and do not allow the sentiment of pity and mercy to become worn out. Pity and mercy may not be statesmanlike, but they are a "divine weakness" and always proved Israel's strength. Mercifulness and loving-kindness are, according to our sages, among the criteria distinguishing the people of Israel. You also know the regular Jewish expression רחמנים בני רחמנים ישראל, "Israel are a compassionate people, the descendants of a compassionate people." You have also heard of the Jewish heart. Do not fail to cultivate these sentiments and to keep them alive among your congregants. Be not so overawed by the sense of organization as to put these great Jewish

virtues into the background.   You can fully hope
for God's mercy even if you commit a sin in this
direction; do not allow your congregants to lose
heart—the Jewish heart.   This Jewish peculiarity
will certainly do no harm to us.

And now, my friends, with these words I will
take leave of you, at least for a time.   My travels
will lead me over two continents, where I shall
probably have occasion to visit many an institution
of Jewish learning and many a training school for
Jewish Rabbis and Jewish teachers.   But I shall
feel proud and easy in my mind when you will give
me reason to think that with whatever obstacles
you may meet, whatever difficulties you will have to
overcome, whatever sacrifices you will be compelled
to make, you will never allow yourself to be led astray
even by heaven or by earth from carrying out this
programme of the great unknown, "Jews we are and
Jews we shall remain."

THE BETH HAMIDRASH.*

I HAVE never realized the force of the Rabbinic interpretation to Psalm 84, verse 8, as this evening. I am referring to the Scriptural words: "They go from strength to strength," which the Rabbis interpret to refer to the man who goes forth from the Synagogue to the Beth Hamidrash, or the House of Learning or the School of Interpretation and Research, to be there occupied in the study of the Torah. But it never struck me so forcibly as when looking upon this complex of buildings arisen within the last few years, comprehending a place of worship, a religious school and a school for teachers. To these has now been added the Beth Hamidrash, forming the goal of religious and intellectual activity; which we are dedicating this evening. In the few remarks I am about to make, I will dwell on the latter.

The author responsible for the term "Beth Hamidrash," to which those who are thirsty for wisdom are invited, is Jesus, the Son of Sirach. He was the first to coin this term, which has become classical in Jewish literature, and we might as well consult him as to the meaning which he attached to it. This we learn from another passage in his book.

*Address delivered at the Dedication of the Dropsie College Building, Philadelphia, Pa., March 11, 1912.

After enlarging upon the men of different trades and handicrafts who "maintain the fabric of the world," but whom he does not give credit for "public counsel" or for "sentence of judgment," he describes his ideal man as follows:

> He is the one that hath applied his soul,
> And meditateth in the law of the Most High;
> He will seek out the wisdom of the ancients,
> And will be occupied in prophecies.
> He will keep the discourses of men of renown;
> And where subtle parables are, he will be there also,
> He will seek out the secrets of grave sentences,
> And be conversant in dark parables.

This, then, the study of the Bible, the cultivation of the wisdom of the ancients, as well as the elucidation of those secret grave sentences, is what constitutes learning and is the purpose for which the Beth Hamidrash is established. Sirach flourished in the second century, B. C. But his conception of learning became a tradition and formed the ideal for thousands of years after him in all Jewish colleges and academies or, as they were called in Hebrew, Botte Midrashoth and Yeshiboth. The only additions made were the productions of the Oral Law which, of course, in the age of Sirach, could not as yet have been a regular object of study.

And this was further, what the founder of this College, Moses A. Dropsie, whose anniversary we commemorate also this evening, arrived at when he described the place in which we are gathered, as an institution created for the purpose of obtaining "ripe scholarship in Hebrew, the Biblical and Rabbinical literature, with which should be connected original investigation and research." This is a Beth Hamidrash in the traditional sense of the word.

The remarkable thing about this will of the late Mr. Dropsie is that, as I understand, it was conceived by him so many years ago, when there hardly existed any Jewish institution in this country which could have suggested to him this idea of original investigation and research. Certainly times have altered in this respect. But when Moses Dropsie began to contemplate his plans which are realized now, we had little thought of higher learning. We erected places of worship of which we can be proud indeed. We built philanthropic institutions which might serve as a model to any community, but we failed to progress to the Beth Hamidrash; we were indifferent to the strength—even religious strength—hidden in original investigation and research, deeming them as devoid of any use for the practical purposes in which we were engaged.

Thank God, we have outgrown this stage and are beginning to be unpractical. The Talmud in defining the character of a city in contradistinction to a village, perceives it in the fact that the former can point to ten men of leisure. The Talmudical term is "Batlanim," but it does not mean lazy or idle people, but, as just indicated, men who are not, by reason of their trade or handicraft, hammering away at the fabric of the world, and who can thus afford to devote themselves to the higher spiritual and intellectual interests of the community. Without a sprinkling of such men, the place may boast of millions of inhabitants, but a village it is and a village it remains. What the

Talmud calls a village, would in modern language
be called provincial, denoting a state of mind narrow
in its horizon, limited in its sympathies and self-
complacently doubting all except its own wisdom and
"hating learning for its own sake." It is just such a
society which is redeemed by these men of leisure.
They certainly lead also an active life—indeed, a
strenuous life. I remember to have read once in the
life of a famous English scholar, in which the remark
occurred that he wished the people who read a learned
book could form some adequate notion of the labor
involved in it. Sometimes a footnote of half a dozen
lines may involve days of study, the consultation of
dozens of volumes, written perhaps in half a dozen
different languages, and the reading of hundreds of
pages which had to be sifted and compressed into a
paragraph or two. Such a life is even more than
strenuous, and it can hardly be appreciated by one
who has never himself tasted either the joys or the
sorrows of research. But it raises the community in
which such impractical men live and where a home
is set apart in which they can follow undisturbed their
intellectual pursuits, out of the narrow and provincial
views of God and man which make us, as a rule, so
petty and so small. But, above all, what they do is
that they teach us how to think, or rather do the
thinking for us. Within recent years we have repeated a good many times the famous phrase, "to do
things." Has it never occurred to you that the time
has come when we should also have a few men at
least who would "think things?" This is the great
mission, to my mind, of universities and colleges,

consisting not so much in the producing of active and practical men, but of men devoted to thinking and contemplation—just men who brood over the "secrets of grave sentences," which sentences, if you examine them closely, you will find not only concern the past, but may also decide for us the fate of our present and future. Such men of the thinking profession dare not be local, for their playground is nothing less than God's world. They may have little to say about town topics or topics of the week, for they treat everything from the point of view of eternity, which includes all time. This is especially the case with the students who are occupied in prophecies. Their extent is the universe both in space and in time. The transient was, according to our ancients, eliminated from the Scriptures, even though it once formed prophecies. "It is the Book of the Generations of Man; embodying a history of Humanity written in advance," as a modern savant expressed it.

And think only of the vast apparatus which is now brought to bear upon the study of the Bible. Whole civilizations, such as the Egyptian, the Assyrian and partly also the Greek, lasting for thousands of years and each ruling in its turn the whole of known humanity, are enlisted by the student of the Bible as auxiliaries of the great document of humanity.

And this great history of the world is constantly expanding when you add to the Bible the post-Canonical productions of Judaism. This is a great literature indeed when you consider its great past, its long history, its affinity with so many schools of thought, Oriental and Occidental, with which it has come into contact during its long career in various countries, its vast jurisprudence, civil and criminal, its tremendous collection of precedents in the Responsa, its liturgy, its poetry, sacred and secular, its devotional and mystic literature, Such a literature not only deserves, but demands the attention of the scholar and the specialist and requires men of leisure, free from all other cares, to teach and to expound it.

But apart from the spoken word, there is also the written word. Whilst the former is represented by the lectures of the professors in the classroom, the latter is given to the world by means of scientific publications. The former can only reach a few, the latter may have the world for its audience. This is the reason that the most representative universities and colleges have their various periodicals or series of publications, to which each department contributes its share. The Dropsie College made a beginning in this direction with the *Jewish Quarterly Review*, which is now in its second year, and which is edited in conjunction with students belonging to other institutions. Its purpose is to advance the cause of Jewish learning in those departments for which neither the regular theological periodicals nor the various other learned societies make sufficient provision. It also endeavors to serve as a model to young students, especially Jewish students, in their scientific work. James Russell Lowell expressed himself once in the following words: "We have a vast amount of imported ignorance and, still worse, of native, ready-made knowledge to digest, before even the preliminaries

of such a consummation can be arranged." The consummation of which Lowell thought was the higher
type of citizenship and freedom. The consummation
which the editors of this *Review* have before their
eyes is that of establishing some standard of the
higher scholarship or of original investigation and
research. Matters may have improved since Lowell's
time. But the Millennium has not yet arrived, and it
is still important to combat all kinds of ignorance,
including "encyclopaedic ignorance"—and to show
that smartness and verbosity which are by some considered a virtue in other walks of life, are not the
instruments with which parables and prophesies of old
are treated. The knowledge of these, or, for that
matter, of any subject worth knowing, can only be
achieved by hard work and exclusive devotion to the
topic in hand and a careful study of the authorities
bearing upon it, written with all the gravity and sense
of responsibility which men bring to bear upon other
questions involving really vital issues. In brief,
we try to train by models of genuine scholarship,
serious scholars and devoted students. I do not belong
to those who think that scholarly work must of
necessity be dull or heavy. We have instances
of brilliant writing and delightful reading furnished
by men who are accepted by the learned world as
the main authorities in their respective subjects.
But brilliancy and delight must not be obtained at
the expense of accuracy and exactness. Moreover,
there are subjects such as grammar, etymology or
questions of chronology and lexicography, or the
collection of *variae lectiones* offered by the collation

of versions and texts which can only be treated in a dry and matter-of-fact manner. Yet they are as indispensable to the philologian as time tables to the traveler. They are not pleasant reading. They are rather disconnected, as somebody said who was studying dictionaries, but you can never reach your destination or the goal of high learning without doing your share of them.

I may further remark that long experience has taught me that the student who has never undergone the discipline given by the editing of an ancient text or the writing of a serious commentary to an ancient classic, where the smallest detail has its meaning, and where even the blunders of the Scribe convey at times most startling lessons, will never acquire that sense of responsibility and scientific conscience which alone go to make the real scholar. Industry and hard reading may enable him to compile a useful manual or readable history of a certain given epoch in modern or ancient times; but there are no elements of permanence in such work. You have always the feeling that you are in the presence of a mere reporter, whom you never take quite seriously and are prepared to abandon altogether as soon as he is contradicted by the next "dealer in information."

Now, I have said that in learned publications it is aimed to have the world as one's audience. But if the world is to share their benefits, these publications have to remain strictly impartial. Pure learning must stand for no party, nor must it have any particular cause to defend. The *Quarterly* remains true to its program and strictly avoids all polemics, though this may rob it of many an incisive or slashing article which would at least enjoy the applause of one party. And it is just because of this strict adherence to the principle of impartiality that this *Review* will in time become the common platform of all parties. Please do not misunderstand me. I am prepared to stand up for my principles and to defend them with all my power. I am grateful to God that I have still some bias in favor of Judaism. I possess nothing of that Mandarin politeness which congratulates a fellowman of a different creed on the superiority of his religion, so much superior to the religion in which he himself was born and bred. I rather congratulate myself in the old manner that I am a Jew. The boast of non-sectarianism in matters of religion does not impress me. In most cases, the man who claims this gift means nothing else but that he forms a Sect for himself. But I have also a strong prejudice in favor of unity, if not among the different sects of the country, at least among the scholars and students of the various colleges and learned institutions in the different sections of the community, longing for some common platform on which they may meet on equal terms in an amicable and brotherly spirit. And this is only possible through such periodicals of pure learning as have no other purposes but to seek and to establish the truth by means of approved scientific method. It is in this manner that this Beth Hamidrash, in conjunction with other Botte Hamidrashoth, or colleges and academies, will prove a real strength. It is only this strength which insures peace in the end.

HUMILITY AND SELF-SACRIFICE AS THE QUALIFICATIONS OF THE RABBI.*

THE occasion for which we have gathered here to-day needs no special explanation. The presence of Faculty and Students in their academic dress tells you at once the purpose of our meeting, though we are not in our own precincts, It is one of those holy convocations which, for many years, has become a regular feature in the community, when degrees are conferred upon and prizes awarded to the students, and Directors and Faculty bear witness to this solemn act. Of late years our Seminary Hall has proved too small to accommodate all those who wished to attend the Commencement Exercises, and it is in deference to public opinion, expressed many a time, that we make our appearance in this Lyceum to-day.

Now, here we are, and if the few remarks which I am about to make, because of the more central location of the place from which I speak, should reach wider circles, I would certainly not object, but they are mainly addressed to my friends, students of the Seminary and students of the Teachers Institute, upon whom the degrees were just conferred.

These remarks suggested themselves to me by the contents of the Scriptural lesson read yesterday.

---

*Address delivered at the Graduating Exercises of the Seminary, June 2, 1912.

As you know, a considerable portion of it dwells upon the subject of the apportioning of elders and leaders in Israel, but I am referring in particular to verses 16 and 17 of the eleventh chapter of Numbers.

> "And the Lord said unto Moses: "Gather unto me seventy men of the elders of Israel, whom thou knowest to be the elders of the people, and officers over them; and bring them unto the tabernacle of the Congregation, that they may stand there with thee. And I will come down and talk with thee there: and I will take of the spirit which is upon thee, and I will put it upon them; and they shall bear the burden of the people with thee, that thou bear it not thyself alone."

My friends, mark well the closing words of the quotation just given: "And they shall bear the burden of the people with thee." I had already once had occasion to quote the words of a Jewish sage in antiquity, bearing on the subject. He was sending out disciples to take up their position in the community. But he warned them that it was service and labor which awaited them, not mastery and dominion. For indeed, they would have to bear the burden and the cares of a whole community. They would be responsible to God and man for their actions, and whatever happens, it is the leader who has in the end to give account and reckoning. "If you see a generation," our sages teach, "which is constantly on the decline, go and investigate the Judges of Israel." And the burden becomes the heavier in a community like ours, in which, because of its youth, the Rabbi has to spend so much time on organization work, and in which this organization becomes doubly heavy and full of obstacles, owing to the heterogeneous elements of which the community is composed. These elements hail from all the corners of the earth, were bred under different conditions, were trained in different schools, each of them possessing its own customs and usages, its own etiquette, and its own ways of thinking, and each of them expecting the leader to be led by them exclusively, and to have no other desires, no other aims, but those sanctioned by them. One of the earliest experiences of Moses was when he beheld two men of the Hebrews who "strove together." The last two words just quoted have become a text with many a mediaeval writer, and they are still striving. Indeed, I think that this is the first experience which any man makes on leaving the academic halls and descending for the first time into the arena of life. Two Hebrews are striving; two sections in the community are striving; two parties in the synagogue are striving; and very often it is more than two. It just depends upon the composition of the community, their antecedents at home, and the variety of homes from which they hail.

My friends, I know that it is hard work to pacify all. But do not forget that the Rabbi is expected to have faith in Israel, even as Moses had. Better times are bound to come, and you are young enough to hope for such times. For your comfort, I will only remind you of Turkish Jewry in the Fifteenth Century or thereabout, which forms the nearest approach to such conditions as you will be called upon to grapple with. The Fifteenth Century was the age of "Pogroms" all over the world, and the newly established Mohammedan Empire in Constantinople was virtually the only one which not only granted the Jew a certain amount of liberty, but practically invited the Jews from all over the world to come there and enjoy these liberties. But they hardly began to settle when the strife began. There were the native Jews who had their own ritual; there were the German immigrants, coming largely from Bavaria, who had also their own ritual; there were the Hungarian Jews, there were the Italian Jews, especially from Sicily, there were the French Jews, especially from the Southern departments; there was also a sprinkling, as it would seem, of Jews from Russia and other Slavonic countries; there were a little later the Spanish, or the Sephardic Jews, but these were also divided into half a dozen rituals, or Minhagim: the Minhag of Aragon, the Minhag of Barcelona; the Minhag of Tudela; and others of which no record has come down to us. And there were also the Jews of Portugal who, though practically coming from the same part of the world as their Spanish brethren, considered themselves as their superiors and held aloof from them. How they quarrelled! They quarrelled over the taxes, as each community had to pay its quota of the tribute to the government; they fought over the ritual, each community insisting on retaining it in its integrity; they quarrelled over the Rabbi, or Preacher or Maggid; sometimes they quarrelled over the so-called "Spreader of the Torah," or head of the College. The Responsa literature of the time is full of such litigations and disputes and controversies. But in a generation or so we see them blending into one large harmonious whole. In the end, higher culture, superior learning and gifted leadership overcome every obstacle. Men arose, great in the Law, great in mystical lore and great also in statesmanship and in philanthropic enterprise. They endowed schools, they erected synagogues, they even established Hebrew presses, and their beneficent influence extended far and wide, creating new centres of Judaism. Great women also contributed their share. It is enough to mention here the names of Donna Gracia Hannah Mendesia, a millionairess, a statesman and a philanthropist on the largest scale, in whom her contemporaries saw Divine Mercy revealed in human form. She is described as "the glory of Israel." She founded schools, she established a Jewish press and devoted herself to deeds of mercy and benevolence which reached even her enemies, "and rescued many of her nation from the depths of endless misery, poverty and sin, led them into safe places, and gathered them together in obedience to the precepts of the true God." Thus they built up the House of Israel anew.

This may happen in this country, too, provided you are animated by the spirit which was upon Moses, which is the spirit of self-sacrifice, and giving yourself up entirely to your work. Moses was the Prophet, as we are told, who gave his very life for Israel, hence the Torah is called after his name: The Torah of Moses. In other words, no message to Israel will

ever succeed in which the messenger thinks less of
Israel and more of himself.

Now, when about to write this address, I was
struck by the following sentence quoted by a famous
author of the last century:

> "At twenty-five," he remarked, "a generous
> soul only seeks to sacrifice its life. It asks of Heaven
> and Earth only a great cause to serve with great
> devotion; love and strength are superabundant."

My friends, you are about the age just described,
perhaps a year or two more or less. You have even
the advantage that you need not seek for a great
cause. Heaven has already assigned this to you.
It is the cause of Judaism, which is great and sacred
enough. But, can we, in our generation, speak with
the same certainty of the generous souls prepared
to sacrifice their lives as the author just mentioned
spoke a century ago? Following the example of
Moses, the injunction given to every man aspiring
to leadership was, "Give your very lives for the community." Have you ever realized that it is this which
is required of you in your sacred calling? The great
misfortune is that we live in a time in which words
and terms have become so stereotyped, so technical,
and so mechanical, that they have become soulless
and meaningless. One is almost inclined to exclaim
with old Johnson, "Sir, free yourself from cant!"
Take the words "sacred calling," as applied to the
Rabbinate. Is it a sacred calling, indeed? Has
it not through faults, not your own, become reduced
to a mere profession, a comfortable office, a snug
berth, in which men spend their lives along a certain

routine. You may call such a career practical and even respectable, but the last thing in the world you can call it is sacred. The old Jews were very sparing with the Hebrew equivalent of sacred, which is קדוש as a rule; when applied to a person, they meant by it a martyr. Are we made of the stuff of which martyrs are made? Do we not rather engage in a profession or accept an office in which martyrdom is more or less out of place? You have given me no reason to doubt your sincerity and readiness for things great. But the spirit of the time may prove too strong for you, so that you may also indulge in phrases which have a very unctuous and solemn sound, but have ceased to mean anything.

Just to take one more example: We constantly speak of ourselves as a nation of Priests and a people with a mission, but we never pause to ask, where are our Priests, and where are our missionaries? Where are our Parishes profiting by our priestly calling? And where are the converts giving evidence of our missionary activity? Now, I frankly confess that I am not in the least troubled by the fact that the Chinese or the Japanese are not yet Monotheists. But we want missionaries for our own people who are constantly drifting away. We want teachers for our own youth to instruct them in the word of God. We want students who will devote themselves to the cause of Jewish learning and continue the work of the old Yeshiboths in a new country, after new methods and with more scientific discipline, if Jewish scholarship is not to disappear altogether. We want Rabbis to organize new congregations and to raise

the old ones from the sloth of indifference and the
vice of strife into which they have fallen. We want
further, as the Rabbis expressed it, men of power and
strength, to grapple with the disintegrating elements
among us, to whatever party they may belong,
whether to those who seek their salvation in levelling
down Judaism to the commonplace of a cheap
universalism or to those who, to use a famous phrase,
"serve the Lord out of spite." And all this can only
be done by young men and young women of "love
and strength in superabundance," forgetting everything, even themselves and having no other cause
at heart but that of Israel.

I have spoken of the office of Rabbi, as one meaning service, not mastery and dominion. The word
"service" need not deter you. It is the highest title
which Judaism knows in connection with your holy
office. "Let Moses rejoice in the gift of his portion;
for thou didst call him a faithful servant." This
feature is closely connected with another, also
mentioned in yesterday's Scriptural lesson. It is
that of עָנְוָה or meekness, or rather humility, which,
according to our Rabbis formed the very calling, or
mission of Moses. It is the spontaneity of action
and suppression of our ego, which does not know when
it shines; indeed, puts on a veil when by some accident it becomes aware of such a possibility of shining.

It is only the man possessing this humility, who
can become the faithful servant of a great idea or
ideal, otherwise he will soon serve himself.

My friends, our earlier Rabbis were in the habit
of saying that it was the terrible and continuous

deprivation caused by constant persecution and
Galuth which has 'devoured many a good quality
among us. I need not dwell on this point. The
truth of this is manifest enough. But I am afraid
that it may equally be true that in modern times it
is the lack of this great quality of humility and the
wish to shine which is the source of no less evils. It
has especially wrought destruction among men who
are about to engage and are engaged in the sacred
calling. We are not satisfied to be the faithful servants, but desire to be the lords and masters. We
wish constantly to shine. Everyone is building an
altar for himself, as the old expression is, and bitterly
resents every attempt towards unity. Whatever
happens, his light must not be put under a bushel,
even though this light may obscure Judaism itself.
He is not the servant of the law, but is constantly
endeavoring to be the lord of the Law. He must
always be in evidence, whether by his strange actions,
or by his peculiar theories. It is almost pathetic to
look upon the craving after publicity which has become so prevalent among us. Some ancient sage
said that every day in which he had not performed a
righteous action, he considered as a lost day. I am
afraid that the sickly craving after publicity has
become such a passion with us that some consider
that every week in their lives in which their names
had not appeared before the public as dead. To
what sensationalism, either in action or in speech,
such a hankering leads, I need not explain.

My friends, remember the word of our sages:
"They will assign to thee what is thine: they will

call you by name and place thee in thy seat. No man
can touch what really belongs to thee, and there is no
forgetfulness with the Omnipresent." The man who
is really in the service of an ideal is not thinking of
himself. Judaism is great enough to fill out all the
heart of man. The service assigned to you is plain
enough; it is to teach Judaism and, as I had occasion
more than once to say: Your teachings must be of
a positive nature, the Jewish Scriptures, the sacred
language, Jewish tradition, Jewish law and ritual,
Jewish doctrine and Jewish history. Polemics should
entirely be avoided. It is the positive statement,
strengthened by the life and devotion of the preacher
which wins the hearts of men in the end. Other subjects, whether un-Jewish or non-Jewish, you had
better leave alone. Make also a point of teaching
Jewish ethics, devotion to the country, devotion to
duty, loyalty, honor, honesty; all these virtues are
taught by Judaism and in Judaism, but do not deceive
yourself that you will help Judaism much by becoming
exponents of topics belonging more to the Lyceum
than to the Synagogue. Above all, bring heart and
enthusiasm into your sacred task. Jewish history
will inspire you with all the enthusiasm you are in
need of. What a wealth of great men and great women
we have had; how courageous they were when it was
a question of religion! Teach your congregants to
admire their devotion, their loyalty and their heroism.
Point out to them what an inheritance we have and
that, as a fact, instead of boasting of our progress,
we are ethically still living in the afterglow of what
we so disdainfully call "Ghetto-Judaism." And
further, point out what will happen when this after-

glow will entirely disappear and darkness will settle
upon our memory and past. To take a modern slo-
gan, "do justice to the Jew," but also to Judaism, to
his history, to his past, and his memories and his
destiny. Do it yourself and do not invite outsiders
constantly to do so. "Justice to the Jew" has become
a regular topic in our papers and our. speeches, and
I am sorry to say that both preachers and laymen indulge a little too much in it. If we are not sufficiently
humble, we ought at least to be too proud for such
things. Can you imagine an ancient Jew, with all
his degradation, inviting strangers to give their
opinions about Jews and Judaism? As far as I had
occasion to observe, such invitations have, as a rule,
the very opposite effect than that expected by those
who solicit these opinions. What happens is something the reverse of what occurred with Balaam. He
was invited to curse, and remained to bless. We
invite them to bless, and not very seldom they curse.
In brief, do not employ artificial means to strengthen
your position in the community. Judaism need not
be advertised. Judaism needs to be taught. It is
not the highest praise for a Rabbi that he is invited
to preach in some church, or that he has succeeded
in procuring some high ecclesiastic or statesman to
preach in his synagogue. If you succeed in getting
the most exalted personage of the United States or
a candidate for the Presidency to preach in your
synagogue, you have only shown your ability of
"doing things," as the phrase is. But have you ever
thought that it does not help Judaism with thoughtful men? It rather reflects upon our sense of religious
delicacy, upon our confidence in our own cause, or

even self-respect. And least of all do such successes in the Rabbinical career give evidence of our devotion to the great Law "to walk humbly before God." You must never forget that even the sermon is not altogether an end in itself. To a certain extent, it is a preparation for prayer, teaching the Congregation to pray and how to pray. As some Rabbi said, "Any homily which cannot be converted into a prayer is a misfit," and this applies both to teaching and preaching.

My friends, I have spoken of the spirit of Moses, but so much abuse has been with the word "spirit," contrasting it with the latter that it will be well that I conclude with the words of the last Prophet: "Remember ye the law of Moses, my servant, which I commanded unto him in Horeb for all Israel, the statutes and judgments."

Remember ye, my friends, Rabbis and teachers gathered here, these "statutes and judgments." It is these statutes and judgments which you have to teach. General phrases about law and legalism are out of place. We have sufficiently indulged in the "recall." It is now the time to build up and to teach positive Judaism and to remember and to remind that the laws and the statues are the very life and substance of Judaism. And this teaching again must be imparted in the spirit of meekness and humility, even as Moses did. And further, remember that it is only the consciousness of being a servant of God, wholly abandoning yourself to the sacred task which is before you which will make your activity a blessing. May the Divine Presence rest upon the work of your hands.

THE ASSISTANCE OF THE PUBLIC.*

THIS is an historical occasion, as we are now to celebrate the tenth commencement of the re-organized Seminary. The occasion is, therefore, an auspicious one. To apply a Scriptural metaphor, "The Tenth shall be holy unto the Lord." And so we have gathered here to confer degrees upon a number of young men who are to devote their life to the sacred calling of the Rabbi, by preaching holiness and all that appertaineth to it.

Historical occasions invite to meditation. The first subject of our meditation shall be the past.

I have spoken of the re-organized Seminary. But it is only meet and proper that on this occasion should be first mentioned the original organization of the Seminary, of which our institution is an outgrowth and a development. Last year, the branch in Philadelphia celebrated the twenty-fifth anniversary of its original foundation, and I had the opportunity to speak of this interesting anniversary in public. By the blessing of God, we have still many of the survivors who were present at the meeting at which the establishment of a new school for the training of Rabbis was first resolved upon. May God prolong their lives to rejoice with all of you at the celebration of the fiftieth anniversary.

But we have especially to recall here some of the

*Address delivered at the Graduating Exercises of the Seminary. June 8, 1913.

names of those who have gone from us. I am thinking
of the Rev. Sabato Morais, the original founder of
this institution, whose saintly character, whose un-
obtrusive piety and whose loyalty to principle will
always remain an inspiring influence in the Seminary;
of Mr. Joseph Blumenthal, as the President of the
Board, who toiled and labored to maintain the
Seminary under the greatest financial difficulties;
and, further, of Dr. Alexander Kohut, who was
just as great as a Rabbi in the pulpit as he was a
Professor in the classroom, and whose connection
with the Seminary, in the capacity of teacher, gave
lustre and standing to our institution. All these
names we record here to-day for good, and their
memory shall not pass away from among those who
are connected with the Seminary in their various
functions and offices.

More difficult I find it to speak of the near
past. I am referring to the last ten or eleven years,
during which I have had the honor to preside over
the Seminary.

I know of nothing more distressing to a man
whose life has been spent mostly in academic surroundings, and who has never been initiated in the
gentle art of self-advertisement, than the occasional
necessity of speaking in public of an institution
for whose activity he is more or less responsible.
However, I imagine that I owe it to my colleagues
and to the Seminary to say a few words also
about this period.

Our work has been a hard one, considering the
want of uniformity in the training of those applying

for admittance, the unenviable conditions of the congregations to which the Seminary has had to appeal
and, finally, the great divisions among the people
engendered by the extreme tendencies of the various
parties, be they Reform or Orthodox, which could
never understand a frame of mind that refused to be
labeled by the names they wished to attach to it.

Now, I do not wish to dwell on details. I shall
not enlarge here on the number of our Rabbis occupying various pulpits—mostly Conservative pulpits—
all over the country; nor on the flourishing condition
of the Teachers' Institute, a regular outgrowth
of the Seminary, which recognized the need of trained
religious teachers long before the public at large
became awake to it; nor shall I take up your time in
giving you a description of our unique library. Suffice
it to say that the Seminary has, with the aid of its
great benefactors, within 'this short space of time,
been able to build up one of the greatest Hebrew
libraries in the world, so that the youngest of the
libraries among Jewish seminaries is now one of the
richest in manuscripts and rare prints.

All these are facts which can be proved statis-
tically. But there are some things more potent than
facts, and these are tendencies and ideals. To be
brief, I will only mention the most prominent of
these. The first was the creation of a conservative
tendency which was almost entirely absent or lay
dormant in this country for a long time. Its aim was
to preserve and to sustain traditional Judaism in
all its integrity and, by means of the spoken or

written word, to bring back to the consciousness of Jewry its heroic past, which must serve as a model, if we would have a glorious future, or any future at all; but, at the same time, to remain in touch with our present surroundings and modern thought, and to adopt what was the best in them and, above all, to make use of modern method and system.

The next step was to create a school of Jewish learning, which should embrace all the departments of Jewish thought, and give it that scientific thoroughness and finish which alone deserves the name of research, as well as enable Judaism to compete with, and to combat those hostile intellectual forces which are often more dangerous to us than pogroms and direct persecution. In both these enterprises, the Seminary has succeeded beyond all hope. The conservative tendency, which recently began only as a mere pious wish, has now become a reality. It permeates all the country and affects (unconsciously, it may be) even those who never tire of scolding us as re-actionaries. As to Jewish learning, it has become a fact. American Jewish scholarship is now a recognized factor all over the world; and you will hardly find at the present time a Jewish library of consequence, whether here or abroad, whether private or public, in which the Seminary is not represented by one publication or another emanating from our faculty.

But we are only at the beginning of our work. The experience of the past ten years, if it has brought to our mind most vividly the nature of the difficulties which we have to conquer, and they are many and great ones, has also opened to us such a wide vista of possibilities and hopes as no other Jewish community has to show. New York itself forms the largest Jewish community recorded in history, while the country in general, with its wise form of government and liberal institutions, is, at present, the only place on our globe where Israel can dwell in security and look forward to a great future. If there is a spot in the world where Jewish learning, which has so often migrated from land to land, should at last find a resting-place and develop freely in accordance with its own laws, it will be America. If the labor will be great, the reward will be greater. To prepare for this future, it will be the duty of the Seminary not only to continue on its path, but even to raise the standard of its program of teaching, and to increase its requirements, both for applicants and graduates. This is the right and the privilege of every progressive institution of learning, after the lapse of a certain period, during which it has fairly taken root in the community.

The desired standard is to be found in the Scriptures. It is given with reference to the first appointment of judges and leaders in Israel, whose mission it was to give decisions to the people who come "to inquire of God." There we read:

> "And thou shalt teach them ordinances and laws, and shalt show them the way wherein they must walk, and the work that they must do."

The second clause of the verse is generally interpreted to refer to the works of "loving kindness," or what we would call social work. But, as you see, the knowledge of the "ordinances and laws" comes first and forms the basis of all. This was the mental equipment of the Judge in Israel who afterwards became the model and standard for all the spiritual leaders of Israel in history. Seminaries can teach ordinances and laws or better, as the original Hebrew has it, "Toroth," a term comprehensive of all Jewish thought, whether deposited in the Scriptures or in the Talmud, whether it finds its expressions in the lessons of Jewish history and Jewish philosophy, or Jewish poetry and Jewish mysticism. It can, further, give some direction in regard to social work, in so far as it is connected with the Torah. But the teaching of the Torah and the spreading of its knowledge is, and will remain, the Seminary's first and paramount duty. I know that we live in a time and under conditions in which social work has become an important factor in the life of our communities, and am sometimes even inclined not to press the question of knowledge to its full claim, when I see in a young man a bent of mind which makes him useful to do, as the phrase is, good work as Rabbi. But we must never lose sight of the *Toroth*, which is the primary object of seminaries. Nor must the Rabbi lose sight of it. And I implore you, my young friends even after you have entered office, never to allow a day to pass without devoting a certain amount of time to the acquiring of the knowledge of the Torah. If it should happen that a certain number among you should be so carried away in the zeal for the Torah, as to engage

in original research, and write some great book on
some Jewish subject, it would certainly not be a
calamity. American Jewry is now strong enough
to afford a few real scholars in the ranks of its clergy.
Such scholars elsewhere prove, as a rule, an ornament
to the church to which they belong, and the Synagogue should not remain behind in this respect.
They are the men who provide their denomination
with ideas and ideals, which are converted into small
cash by the weaker brethren before they reach the
public. There is room in the Synagogue for all sorts
and conditions of Rabbis, but the rabbi-scholar must
not be allowed to disappear if Judaism is not to be
reduced to the straits of a mere ranting sect, if our
places of worship shall not become settlement houses
in disguise, and our seminaries mere sociological
institutions. In Judaism, everything must emanate
from the Torah and culminate in it. We cannot
live entirely for the fleeting moment. We have duties to
the past and to the future, and these duties can only
be accomplished by raising the standard of knowledge
of the Torah in the Rabbinate. To achieve this end,
we must, however, have the assistance of the public.
As you have observed in the citation given from Exodus, this command as to the qualification of the judges
was given in answer to a need felt by a people "coming to inquire of God." Unless such a need is felt in
our times, the Seminary will never be able to do its
full duty. The public must feel the need of a learned
rabbi, so as to enable us to increase the years of study
in our institution. There must be a demand for the

knowledge of laws and statutes, in other words, of
the Torah, and all that appertains to it, so as to give
the better scholar the better opportunity in life and
the greater field for his work. The Jewish public
must begin to show this interest in its learned institutions and aid it in its task by the material and moral
support, which it has always shown to philanthropic
institutions. If the Seminary is to develop on the
lines begun thus far, it is absolutely necessary that
it should have the disposition of larger means than
hitherto. Thus, it is important that a "publication
fund" should be created, enabling the faculty to give
to the world annually, at least, a volume or two of
scientific production. We want also more scholar-
ships and more valuable ones that would enable us
to keep the student for some longer period in the
Seminary. The age at which young men are now sent
out to conduct the spiritual affairs of congregations
is certainly too early and is against all precedent.
We want Fellowships to encourage original research
among our alumni, immediately after graduation.
We have men who give great promise in this regard,
but we are unfortunately not in a position to enable
them to continue their researches without immediately
taking up practical work. We want, further, dormi-
tories for our students. The longer I live in this
country and the more familiar I become with the
conditions, economic as well as spiritual, the more
convinced I am that such an arrangement is absolutely necessary to make the work of the teachers
effective, and the life of the students fairly comfortable.

It is high time that American Jewry should recognize the claims of the Jewish student, generally called in Jewish literature, "the Sons of the Torah." Thus far, we have treated them as step-sons. It is only by the co-operation of the public and their sympathy with the student and his work that a knowledge of the Torah will again become the criterion of the Rabbi, that religious education will become effective as it should be, and that harmony and mutual understanding will be brought about in the various sections of the community. Or, to speak in biblical language, forming the conclusion of the passage quoted from Exodus:

"If thou shalt do this thing and God command thee so, then thou shalt be able to endure and all this people shall also go to their place in peace."

HIS MAJESTY'S OPPOSITION.*

A T THE request of the Board of Directors of
the Jewish Theological Seminary of America,
at the wish of my colleagues, as well as following my
own inclination, I have come here to offer you our
congratulations on this auspicious occasion, the dedication of the new buildings of the Hebrew Union
College. It is a pleasure to me to have seen this great
edifice with its commodious halls, its well-equipped
library and its fine classrooms, erected to the glory
of God, and at the same time forming a monument
sacred to the memory of the late Dr. Isaac M. Wise,
the founder of this Institution. I remember to have
read once, in a book by an early American writer,
who complained of the want of distinguished men in
this country, and of the lack of reverence to the few
great names we do possess. These buildings, bearing
the name of one of the leaders of Reform Judaism
in America, removes this reproach. It shows that we
are now beginning to learn the meaning of reverence
and authority, for even Reform Judaism cannot live
without authority.

I here take the opportunity of putting on record
my thanks to the family of the late Dr. Isaac M. Wise.
I had not the honor of knowing the head of the family,
who had already been taken from us before I removed
to this country, but I had the pleasure of making the

*Address delivered at the Dedication of the new Hebrew Union
College Buildings, Cincinnati, Ohio, January 22, 1913.

acquaintance of Mrs. Wise very soon after my arrival in America. And I acknowledge here with thanks that both she and her sons, as well as other members of the Wise family, always treated me with uniform kindness and attention. And this in spite of all my heresies regarding Reform Judaism and other theological frailties symptomatic of my want of sympathy with reform tendencies, of which I have never made any secret.

My pleasure is not spoiled by hearing and seeing so much here from which I of necessity differ. Indeed, if I were in agreement with you, I would have been deprived of the pleasure of being here today; at least, in the capacity of President of another college pursuing, to a certain extent, different aims and endeavoring to realize them by largely different methods. Least of all would I, a mere student, without the least forensic ability, have a right to speak in this distinguished gathering consisting of so many great scholars and orators, as your illustrious President and other Rabbis here who have grown old in the service of the Synagogue and famous for their gifts of oratory and speech. But there is also another consideration. Probably you all know the way in which some English statesmen speak of their opponents in the Parliament, referring to them as His Majesty's Opposition. This sounds like a paradox, yet it contains a deep truth, implying as it does that both His Majesty's government as well as His Majesty's opposition form one large community, working for the welfare of the country and the prosperity of the nation. The same principle may also be applied to theology, there being, under Providence, room also for the opposition party, which has its purpose and mission assigned to it by history. Of course, there are exceptions, but generally there is hardly any phenomenon in Judaism in the way of sect or movement which has not served a certain purpose in the divine economy of our history.

For opposition there must be, owing to the difference of temper and temperament, the difference of training, the difference of surroundings which no process of schooling can entirely obliterate, and the difference of opportunity. Of course, it will always be a question as to which is which; we Conservatives maintaining that we are His Majesty's Government and you His Majesty's Opposition. But this is one of the differences. For reduce your differences as much as you want, and, indeed, I hope and pray that the difference of aims is not so deep as we sometimes think, the fact remains that we are unfortunately divided both in questions of doctrine—at least certain doctrines—and even more in practice. But, thank God, there are still a great many things and aims for which both parties can work in perfect harmony and peace, and unite us. To mention here only two: There is, first, the question of Jewish learning, which concerns us all. This, as has often been pointed out, can only be accomplished by the Jews and for the Jews. No outsider can do it for us even when representing the most liberal point of view, for there is such a thing as a Jewish liberalism and a non-Jewish liberalism, as my friend, the learned President of this College, knows as well as I. To this, any student keeping pace with the productions of theology, philosophy and history will bear evidence. We have thus to do our scholarship for ourselves. I had only lately an experience of this fact. In the course of my studies I found it necessary to read a certain book dealing with the geography of Eastern Europe in the tenth century. You would think that with such a book on such a neutral subject one might feel safe. But it was full of venom and hatred giving evidence to the anti-Semitic tendencies of the author. The most amusing thing was that the subject of his special attack in whom he discovered so much Rabbinical confusion and Talmudic aberrations, etc., was Paulus Cassell, who became converted to Christianity some fifty years ago. But there is a practical side to this question, touching also the larger Jewish public. I am thinking especially of the problem of text-books for our teachers of religious schools and educated laymen. At present we recur to works written or compiled by Christian authors. This must not be allowed to continue. This class of books, which should have the purpose of imbuing our children with loyalty and devotion and attachment to Judaism, should be composed by ourselves. Christian works on the same line will not help us to bring up our children as Jews. We cannot have our love letters written for us. We must write them ourselves, even at the risk of bad grammar. And this is a work in which both parties, realizing the nature of the problem, can work together.

This is a specimen of work for the Jew and by the Jew. But there is also the great work which Judaism can do for humanity at large, in which both parties can combine. It is only sufficient to mention here the

terrible atrocities perpetrated under the eyes of
Europe in the Near East. Men, women and children,
all non-combatants, are slaughtered by the thousands
every day, their number amounting to half a million
already, according to the estimate of the newspapers.
And yet, no real moral indignation is seen anywhere.
We simply put away our papers and enjoy our break-
fast as if nothing had happened. We have become so
infatuated with the doctrine of the survival of the
fittest that we have lost all sensibility to the great
moral catastrophes which are passing before our very
eyes. And the more philosophy, the more heartless
we become. The world is thus in need of new instruction, and this instruction, as history has taught at
various epochs, as, for instance, in the Reformation,
can only come from the Old Testament.

The Fatherhood of God has always been taught
by Judaism, but this is a time in which the aspect of
the Holy King, and the King of Judgment, who not
only reigns, but governs, should be emphasized. As
my friend, Dr. Kohler, has expressed himself in his
recent very interesting essay on the subject: *Die
Naechstenliebe in Judenthum*:

"Nun, ich moechte als Theologie die Liebe nicht
missen, aber ich verlange als Jude, erst Gerechtigkeit
und dann Liebe."

("As theologian, I should not like to miss the
principle of love, but as a Jew I expect first justice
and afterwards love.")

These great principles of God's holiness, God's
justice and God's governing the world, are to be
especially taught now. And they must be taught

for years and years to come.   The whole of Jewish
literature forms a commentary to it; the whole of
Jewish history forms an illustration of it; the whole
of Jewish life should bear evidence to it.   And in
this work we can all combine in teaching.   But in
order to teach, we must first learn and practice.
And this is the purpose for which colleges are established.   And thus may God's blessing be upon this
College, among all other colleges of Catholic Israel
כלל ישראל, in which these great truths of Judaism
shall be taught and learned, and then proclaimed to
the world, in all their purity and in all their application to the different and various departments of life
and thought.

In conclusion, I wish also to thank Dr. Kohler, the
President of this College, as well as all those gathered
here, for the kind reception which has been accorded
me.   I was really touched by the honor you have
shown me.   May God reward you for this act of
Gemillath Chasadim.   "For my brethren and com-
panions' sakes, I will now say, Peace be within thee.
Because of the house of the Lord our God I will seek
thy good."

"LOVINGKINDNESS AND TRUTH."*

M Y FRIENDS:—It is a source of great pleasure to me to be with you on this auspicious day, a privilege which was denied to me last year. For this change in my condition, I am deeply grateful to Almighty God, who kept me alive and has preserved me and enabled me to reach this season.

My first duty would be to congratulate you on behalf of the Faculty and myself on this great occasion, which enables you to enter on the sacred calling of Rabbi. The nature of this sacred calling has been sufficiently discussed in the class rooms. Every lecture delivered there, whether it be on the Sacred Writ and its commentators, or on the Talmud and its cognate literature, or on historical documents and philosophic and theological works by Jewish thinkers, ought to have impressed you with the magnitude of your task and the solemn character of your responsibility. It is a peculiar world into which we have endeavored to introduce you. This world, generally called Judaism, sometimes also, to take a somewhat more concrete term, the Synagogue, is a world within a world, or rather a Sanctuary, symbolizing as the Tabernacle of old, Creation and the Universe, even whilst its long wanderings through the "Wilderness of the nations," renders it a veritable epitome of the history of mankind. The Torah is the "Book of the

* Address delivered at Commencement Exercises of the Jewish Theological Seminary, June 6, 1915.

Generations of Man" or "The history of mankind written in advance;" whilst the great Hebrew Rabbinic literature developing from it, forms the contemporary chronicle of the noblest and the most sublime thoughts of Israel during the long period following the conclusion of the Canon. But as with the Levites of old, it is upon you to carry on the service of the Sanctuary, to make its symbolism intelligible to the laity, to perpetuate its history, and to preach to the world at large its ideals and aspirations.

And now, a glance at the present and the immediate future. We live in awful times. It is a world in conflagration. We cannot divert our eyes from it. We dare not remain indifferent. Any man, to whatever party he may belong, whatever his descent may be, who does not, when reading his morning or evening paper, feel sometimes as if his heart would break at this terrible suffering of humanity—in which Israel is the greatest sufferer among the nations—must, to say the least, be classed among those whom the late Mr. Gladstone described as having come into the world with a "double dose of the original sin." The situation can only be depicted in the words of the Prophet: "Blood and fire and pillars of smoke," preceding the great and terrible Day of the Lord. An ancient Jew would have perceived in it the travail of the universe, ushering in the rebirth of the world, or to use a term which is now greatly in vogue, the regeneration of humanity. What shape this regeneration will take is difficult to say; but if all signs are not deceiving, if the world is not to sink under its own burden, if humanity is not to witness such a reversion to chaos as followed the breakdown of the Roman Empire, and similar world catastrophes—then it will not be in the direction of the religion of valor. It will be a return to the religion of Israel, whose great invocation in the most solemn prayer of the most solemn day of the year is "The Lord, the Lord God, merciful and gracious, long suffering and abundant in lovingkindness and truth." ורב חסד ואמת

My friends, it will be a chastened humanity which will emerge from a destroyed world, strewn with the *debris* of broken idols and shattered ideals on which we have been spending our energies for the last decades. Strength, force, astuteness and similar virtues, desirable in themselves as manifestations of vigorous manhood but dangerously bordering on violence and brutality, will be less valued than meekness, gentleness, sweetness of disposition and humility. It will not be the strong man, but the good man, the affectionate man, who will form the desired goal of parents and pedagogues. Organization itself, this great achievement of our age, will largely give way to generous impulses and broad sympathies. I by no means underrate the value and the importance of organization. It certainly turns mobs into societies and societies into powerful units. It is for the adult what method and system are for the young in the school. But it can decidedly be overdone, and if not under the control of a strong moral principle, touched by kindness and goodness, modifying the severity and its tendency to inconsiderateness, it is more likely to further passion than compassion.

The same is true of efficiency, which has constantly
to be qualified by fitness. To give an illustration
or two: A letter in the papers forming a part of the
controversy about a certain religious leader much
in evidence now, bore the heading, "Coarse, but
shows Results." Here you have a case of efficiency
lacking in fitness, with a vengeance. To speak of
Rabbis in particular: it may happen that the Rabbi
is successful in attracting large audiences, and in
having every pew of his synagogue sold, and in seeing his name in the press every day of the week.
This may be termed efficiency. But if he is not at
the same time a God-fearing man, an observer of the
Jewish law, living an unselfish life, and giving evidence of his humility and meekness, he is certainly
unfit for his calling, and all his activity will result
in destruction.

Above all will this regeneration be felt in the
Synagogue. The pulpit will cease to be an institution of self-glorification, boasting of our successes
in various departments of secular endeavor. This is
sufficiently done by our friends outside of the Synagogue, and even more often by our open and disguised enemies, such as Werner Sombart in his
book, "The Jew and Capitalism," or John Foster
Fraser in his "The Conquering Jew."

Nor must we indulge in emphasizing too much
the question of our mission. Such topics are only
provoking of criticism. To have a mission, but never
to be able to point to the missionaries and their
achievements, is an awkward position to say the least.
I would not even advise you to enlarge too frequently
on the feature of nationalism. It is certainly justi-

fied as a protest against Paulinistic tendencies or
as a safeguard against assimilation. But the most
sublime expressions of Jewish nationalism are to be
found in the Bible and the Prayer Book. Here a
specimen from the latter, "O·Guardian of an only
nation, guard the remnant of an only nation, and suffer
not an only nation to perish, who proclaim the unity
of Thy name, saying, 'The Lord our God, the Lord
is One.' " But the nationalism of the purely secular
kind as taught by certain philosophers and historians
within the last two generations leading to the excesses
which we are witnessing now all over the world had
better be relegated to the lecture platform. Jewish
nationalism can be interpreted only in the light of
Jewish History and pure Jewish thought. Moreover,
the world is sure to combine against the fanaticism of
modern Chauvinism just as it did combine in the
eighteenth century against religious fanaticism. And
Judaism should ponder deeply before it entirely
identifies itself with this sort of exaggerated secular
nationalism. An ancient Jewish moralist had the
maxim: "If you are in the humor of praising, praise
God; if you are in the frame of mind of blaming,
blame yourself." And I am certain that the time
has come when this maxim will be applied as much
to whole groups of humanity as to individuals.
Jewish nationalism is holy to the Lord, and any attempt to sever it from the historical Jewish ideals
attached to the Biblical terms "God's People," or
a "Holy Nation," will fail in the end.

חסד (Chesed) loving-kindness, and אמת (Em-
eth) truth, must again become the subjects of instruction in our places of worship. The great truth

in need of being realized at the present crisis is the fact of sin. Once more we should repeat the formula of the liturgy: "Verily *we* have sinned." I lay the emphasis on *we*, as certain views are now in the air recalling to our minds the Scriptural adage:

> "The foolishness of man perverteth his way; and his heart fretteth against the Lord." (Prov. 19:3.)

We do not fret directly against the Lord, but we fret against religion. "Religion is a failure, else this terrible catastrophe would never have occurred." This is the statement made on all sides. But is it religion that is a failure? Have we been living in a really religious age when this calamity overwhelmed us? Has there been any doctrine which has remained unassailed during the last two generations; any portion of the Scriptures, which has escaped heartless dissection; any religious symbol or ceremony which was not slighted more or less? Almost every ideal sanctioned by tradition and the consent of humanity has been boldly challenged, whilst many a noble sentiment almost inherent in the race and taken for granted by humanity at large, has been ridiculed and looked upon as an impediment to the perfection of a misunderstood manhood. "Everybody at all familiar with the trend of thought could feel that *we're* standing on a veritable volcano created by the upheavals of the newest methods of "searching research" which respects as little the new formulae, such as the categoric imperative and conscience, as it does creeds and dogmas." And now, when all the sources of our inspiration had been destroyed and laid dry, we expected religion to quench this world conflagration. The wife of Job, as you know, said to her husband, "Curse God and die!" We blasphemed religion and wanted to live. It proved impossible. It is this truth that it has been *we* who have been the failure, not religion, which it will be your duty as Rabbis in Israel to impress upon your Congregations.

Where we mainly failed was in the attribute of חסד (Chesed). When speaking of Chesed, I am thinking of the term in all its connotations—kindness, loving-kindness, goodness, mercy, affection, pity, piety, forbearance, gentleness, gracefulness and graciousness. It is this Chesed as an emanation of the Divine, which should become the prominent feature in all our great Jewish enterprises. Charity, for instance, must not be allowed to be converted into a mere department of Political Economy. I have read lately an article under the title of "Humanizing our Charities." But humanizing alone will not suffice. Charity must be restored to its pristine Divine right, the only Divine right which a democracy recognizes, and should be allowed to call forth tll those noble impulses in man which may be summed up as the *Imitatio Dei* of the Jew. If our philanthropic work cannot for practical reasons any longer form a part of the activity of the Synagogue, as it was in days of yore, it must not on the other hand be allowed to become so detached from all religion as to obscure entirely the feature of Chesed or the religious touch which sanctifies the giver and elevates the recipient. Indeed, the great danger of our age is the tendency towards secularizing life and thought in all its aspects, even those aspects which originated in the Sanctuary, grew up with the Sanctuary, and thrived under its shelter from time immemorial. The Sacred Writ, it is maintained, is to be studied as a mere ancient classic, not as a Torah of חסד (Torath Chesed) a gift to Israel by Divine grace. Religion is to be taught as a part of Hebraic culture, not as a discipline of life for the sake of God or Torah lishmah. Jewish endeavor in the line of Jewish settlements and kindred social work is to be conducted on non-religious lines, a peculiar sort of neutrality, but certainly not a friendly neutrality. Silence in religion means hostility. The synagogue itself, affectionately called by our ancestors מקום קדוש (Makom Kadosh) a Sacred Place, is to be largely stripped of its sacred features. It is to make room for the Institutional Synagogue in which the worship of God by reason of its organization must become in the end subordinated to the material service of man and his amusements.

It is this constant encroaching upon the rights of the Sanctuary, leaving no room for the sacred and the holy, which landed us in a materialism, the consequences of which are only visible now. Chesed is banished from the world. It is a world without pity and without piety. The task of the Rabbi as the guardian of the Sanctuary, is to cry a halt to these encroachments, and to restore the Sanctuary to its own rights. The task will not be easy, and the less so as such a restoration of the sacred and holy in our midst would imply a censure of many an activity of ours as not less a subversion of many a philosophy bearing upon man and his destiny in which we have revelled until now. As Lincoln expressed it in his famous letter to Thurlow Weed with reference to his Second Inaugural Address, forming practically a confession of the national sin: "I believe," he wrote, "it is not immediately popular. Men are not flattered by being shown that there has been a difference of purpose between the Almighty and them." But you must do your duty even at the risk of not pleasing everybody. The rights of the Sanctuary are clear. Its province is sufficiently marked, and its mission at this time is sufficiently urgent.

The world cannot exist without a Sanctuary and cannot live without Chesed, even as it is said: "Surely goodness and mercy shall follow me all the days of my life, and I will dwell in the House of the Lord forever."